The Consultative Approach

About Advance Consulting, Inc.

We began Advance Consulting in 1990 with the mission of advancing the way people and organizations work. Our focus is on enabling professionals to work more effectively with internal and external clients by broadening their expertise and by developing their partnering and consultative skills. Following is Advance Consulting's suite of performance improvement workshops and related consulting services:

Workshops	Consulting Services
The Consultative Approach	Consultative culture development
Managing Client Interactions	Transition management
Focused Coaching	Project team building
Building Relationships Through Partnering	Implementation consulting
The Consultative Meeting	Customer team building

For more information about Advance Consulting, Inc. and our products and services, contact us at (415) 435-3001 or write to:

Advance Consulting, Inc., 582 Virginia Dr., Tiburon, CA 94920

We can be reached by e-mail at:

advanceinfo@advanceconsultinginc.com}

The Consultative Approach

Partnering for Results!

Virginia LaGrossa
Suzanne Saxe

Published by Pfeiffer
A Wiley Imprint
989 Market Street, San Francisco, CA 94103-1741 www.pfeiffer.com

The authors have applied to trademark the following phrases and graphics: "The Consultative Roles," "The Consultative Approach," "Advance Consulting," "People, Process, Expertise," the Consultative Roles jigsaw puzzle graphic, the Advance Consulting logo, and the Consultative Balance graphic.
Quotes by Frank A. Clark in Chapter Two, Dean Rusk and Charles F. Kettering in Chapter Five, and Cesare Pavese in the Part Two text are reprinted with permission from *The Great American Bathroom Book*, Salt Lake City: Compact Classics, 1992.

Limit of Liability/Disclaimer of Warranty: While the publisher and author have used their best efforts in preparing this book, they make no representations or warranties with respect to the accuracy or completeness of the contents of this book and specifically disclaim any implied warranties of merchantability or fitness for a particular purpose. No warranty may be created or extended by sales representatives or written sales materials. The advice and strategies contained herein may not be suitable for your situation. You should consult with a professional where appropriate. Neither the publisher nor author shall be liable for any loss of profit or any other commercial damages, including but not limited to special, incidental, consequential, or other damages.

Readers should be aware that Internet Web sites offered as citations and/or sources for further information may have changed or disappeared between the time this was written and when it is read.

Pfeiffer books and products are available through most bookstores. To contact Pfeiffer directly call our Customer Care Department within the U.S. at 800-956-7739, outside the U.S. at 317-572-3986, or fax 317-572-4002.

Pfeiffer also publishes its books in a variety of electronic formats. Some content that appears in print may not be available in electronic books.

Acquiring Editor: Larry Alexander
Developmental Editor: Susan Rachmeler
Copyeditor: Marcella Friel
Director of Development: Kathleen Dolan Davies
Senior Production Editor: Dawn Kilgore
Manufacturing Manager: Becky Carreño
Cover Design: Paula Schlosser

Library of Congress Cataloging-in-Publication Data

LaGrossa, Virginia.
    The consultative approach : partnering for results!
  Virginia LaGrossa and Suzanne Saxe. — 1st ed.
      p. cm.
    Includes bibliographical references and index.
    ISBN 0-7879-1100-3
    ISBN 978-0-470-43197-9 (paperback)
    1. Management—Employee participation. 2. Corporate culture.
  I. Saxe, Suzanne. II. Title.
  HD5650.L25 1998   97-47050
  658.3'152—dc21

10 9 8 7 6 5 4 3 2 1

CONTENTS

To our parents and life partners

ACKNOWLEDGMENTS

This book is the result of the love, support, and patience of our families and friends, the generous advice and encouragement from colleagues, and the vision and innovation of our clients. Since 1988 we have been researching, experimenting with, and refining The Consultative Approach through our client work. To all our clients we have been honored to be a part of your vision and growth. Many receive special thanks:

- The team at Arthur Andersen, who have been so generous with ideas, time, and encouragement: Kristin Andress, Sue Bumpass, Steven Cornejo-Garcia, Jane Creen, Oliver Cummins, Susan Gawley, Marshal Gerber, Mary Johnson, Marsha Johnston, Jon Olson, Beth Piper, Harry Ruffalo, and Jeff Totten. Thanks for your support over the years.

- International Network Services: John Drew, Doug Gabbert, Tod Grantham, Pete Licata, Harold Long, Don McKinney, Frank Musacchia, Jon Rolph, Ralph Troupe, Steve Umphreys, and Nan Watanabe. We have loved working with you to develop a consultative culture as you grew into a leading network services company.

- Laura Penland and Steven Weiner of Science Applications International Corporation, Commercial Health Care, for the opportunity to work with you and your division.

- The Corporate Human Resources department at Bank of America for having us be part of developing consultative skills. Special thanks to Kirsten Alston, John Lingvall, and Nancy Raymond.

- Gary Cooper, Judy Estey, Mike FitzGerald, Sossi Keuylian, and Thomas Smith at CB Commercial, whose vision and talents proved that working consultatively in a fast-paced and individualistic sales environment creates results.

- Art Feather of Cisco Systems, we appreciate the opportunity to work with you and your consulting team.

We owe immense gratitude to all of the people who have attended our workshops throughout the world and have shared their experiences and stories with us. We thank those who responded to our follow-up surveys or were interviewed. Your experiences in working consultatively were invaluable, and we regret that we could not fit all of them into the book. But you are here in spirit!

We thank our associates, colleagues, and friends who have supported us in this endeavor and given invaluable amounts of feedback throughout the years: Keith Bailey, Mia Benedict, Joyce Bennett, Joanne Black, Maureen Burkley, Diane Egelston, Yvonne Ellison-Sandler, Craig Garshelis, Susan Gatten, Barbara Heffernan, Greg Ketchum, Judy Kirkpatrick, Karen Leland, Tom Masiello, Carole McCormick, Mary Jo Potter, Karen Russo, Laura Russo, Susan Strasburger, and Jean Westcott.

As our manuscript developed, we depended greatly on numerous people's talents: Paula Doubleday for her graphic and information design both in the manuscript and in our workbooks throughout the years; Michelle Jordan for her research, feedback, editing, and fabulous job at managing client services for Advance Consulting; Marilyn Cossey for her attention to details and for taking such good care of Advance Consulting's business records; Lynda McGlone, who managed all the details of securing permission for quotes, stories and references and still got all of her other work done too; Jennifer Wengler for her swiftness and accuracy in working with messy drafts; Laura Daly for her editing talents and marketing savvy; Andy Pasternack for reviewing our proposal, and Ellen Pasternack for introducing us to Andy; Susan Rachmeler, our editor, for guiding us through this process with professionalism and a great sense of humor; Leslie Tilley for masterfully honing our words with little direction in an incredibly short time frame.

Most of all, we want to thank each other for maintaining a true sense of partnering from the conception to the birth of the book. Our personal and professional growth from this experience can only be described as phenomenal.

VIRGINIA'S PERSONAL ACKNOWLEDGMENTS

This book could not have been written without the love, understanding, and graphic talents of Paula Doubleday, my partner in life. A huge thanks for taking care of the day-to-day stuff in our lives, so that I could concentrate on this effort. Smiles to Sadie, Charlotte, Scout, Beamer, and Gray Cat for reminding me that getting away from it was important, too. To Jean Roux, thanks for your love and patience in helping Suzanne and me as authors, as partners, and as people.

To my parents, Jim and Jeanne LaGrossa, who after fifty-two years of marriage are my role models for practicing partnering every day, whose endless energy must have rubbed off on me somehow, and who taught me at an early age through their example to live life as an adventure. To my sisters Linda, Camille, Leslie, and Alyson and their families for their love and support, especially since I am far away in distance but not in their hearts.

To Liz Adams, Susan Gatten, Judy Kirkpatrick, Sandy Miller, Ellen Pasternack, Mary Jo Potter, Chris Rider, Kim Rothstein, and Barbara Vick for being dear friends when I most needed you.

To all my friends and members of the medical community who contributed to my recovery to full health and vigor. You profoundly changed my life.

And last, thanks to Veda Cowan, who graded my papers and helped me understand the writing process as a labor of love.

SUZANNE'S PERSONAL ACKNOWLEDGMENTS

Many people have supported me in this journey and in the writing of this book.

First, I thank my husband, Jean Roux, for all his support, encouragement, and nourishment of my mind and soul. Thanks to Jasper for staying by my side into the wee hours. And to Virginia's partner, Paula Doubleday for her encouragement, love and support.

To my father, Jerry Saxe, who twenty-one years ago named himself "partner" when his first grandson was born. He is the epitome of what it means to be a partner in life to all who have the great opportunity to work with him and be with him. My mother, Marilyn Saxe, deserves a special thanks for continuing to encourage me in the creative process of writing this book. Thanks to my sisters, Bari and Cynthia, their dear families, and the Roux family, who always provided love and support.

To my Grandma Rose, who died at ninety-nine during the writing of this book, I attribute my stamina to her good genes and her mottos: "You can always sleep when you're dead" and "Make the most of every moment." Grandma, rest in peace.

Without the life-long support of many friends and family members this book would have remained in the bookshelf of my mind. The philosophical and psychological support I received from my dear friends has been an inspiration: Kirsten Alston, Peggy Askew, Don Bauer, Kathy Collard-Bauer, Roxanne Howe-Murphy, Anne Idema-Albano, Shelley C. Katz, Carrie Messina, Jim Murphy, Darcey Sears, and Mark and Debbie Spohr. Thanks from the bottom of my heart to my other friends and colleagues, too many to name.

Partnering

When you engage in some activity in common with another,
You are players on the same side, you are partners with each other.

Working together, pulling together, being a co-worker and a teammate,
Whatever you call it, you are never second rate.

When you do your job, do it with finesse,
And you shall see partnering is a success.

—Jerry Saxe

INTRODUCTION

Partnering for Results

Over the past ten years, something profound has happened to the way people work. Everyone from management to manufacturing has found that their jobs demand more from them—and not just more time or effort but new skills and new abilities.

You yourself—like many professionals—may have found that suddenly your job function has been redefined. You're expected to provide greater value to your clients or customers while (of course) you continue to do what you've always done: use your expertise and organizational knowledge to get the job done, solve problems, and stay within budget and on schedule.

It's no longer enough simply to supply your expertise; you must present and use it in the way that best answers the customers' needs. And this in turn means working with other people—team members, subject matter experts, end users, financial people—to find out what that way *is*. For most people, all of this requires a new set of skills and a totally different mind-set. In other words, meeting today's challenges means fundamentally changing the way you work.

It is often observed that technology such as e-mail, pagers, cell phones, and such has changed the way we work. It has certainly increased the quantity of business (and personal) communication—but it's done little to improve the quality. The "technology" we offer in this book is intended to address that deficit. The techniques presented here will help you develop the consultative and partnering skills you need to work effectively with others and thus provide greater value to your customers. They will give your expertise greater impact and ensure that you continue to be seen as a valuable resource in your organization.

WHAT IS THE CONSULTATIVE APPROACH?

In the workshop series that this book grew out of, we define *The Consultative Approach* as "partnering with others to produce optimum results and simultaneously build trust and commitment." Working consultatively—as a partner—

enables you to produce the best results possible under the circumstances while developing a mutually beneficial relationship with clients.

We began developing the tools, techniques, and skills presented in *The Consultative Approach* in 1989 in response to our clients' need to cope with the changing workplace. Layers of management were being removed. People were expected to function more autonomously and to work on projects and in teams rather than simply filling a job. In effect, they were being asked to act more as consultants than employees, and they didn't yet know how to go about it. It was a painful transition for many people, and we believed we could help them through the process.

The methodologies we use are drawn from disciplines such as consulting, sales, project management, education, communication, and psychology. Through our workshop series, professionals from various industries have learned these skills and applied them to expand their expertise and achieve significant, measurable results. These professionals have changed the way they work and have become true business partners to their clients and customers.

One of our clients, Steven Weiner, a deputy program manager at Science Applications International Corporation, describes the effect the workshop had on his employees: "After they began to work consultatively, I noticed an improvement in employees' listening abilities. They used to listen for content only. They were great note-takers. Now, they also listen to develop rapport and to understand the larger issues. They try to put themselves in their customers' shoes. The results are dramatically different."

WHAT DOES IT MEAN TO WORK CONSULTATIVELY?

There are three critical dimensions to working consultatively:

1. Knowing how to work effectively with all types of people
2. Using a strategic and collaborative process
3. Applying your expertise in ways that show your value

Working consultatively means keeping these three elements in balance.

We all know experts who are vastly knowledgeable but who, unfortunately, no one wants to work with for very long. So how much value do they really add? They are tolerated only as long as their knowledge remains unique. One of our clients, who outsources a considerable amount of work, shared this story with us: "We have this consultant working with us on a project. He is very knowledgeable in his field, but acts like he knows everything. I'm managing the project day to day and need to be included in decisions, but he doesn't treat me as a partner, so I inherently distrust him. Recently he sent me an invoice, and because of the way I feel about working with him, I questioned every line item. I'll be so glad when this project is over!"

In essence, being consultative requires you to balance your people skills, your most efficient work processes, and your role and expertise in the work or project. We call this the Consultative Balance, and it looks like this:

Too much emphasis on any one element causes an imbalance somewhere else—and dissatisfaction in the overall outcome. We return to the Consultative Balance in Chapter One and examine it in greater detail.

OVERVIEW OF THE BOOK

The eleven chapters of *The Consultative Approach* are divided into four parts, each of which builds on the last. Part One presents the most fundamental skills and techniques that make up The Consultative Approach. In Chapters One through Three you will learn how to think and act as a partner. You will identify various client groups, gain insights from observing interactions with them, and learn how to build better rapport. Finally, you will acquire techniques for presenting your expertise to clients in the way that means the most to them and for expanding your expertise into other areas that will add value.

In Part Two you will be introduced to a framework and a variety of techniques for managing interactions. Every interaction, whether a formal meeting or a quick phone call, can move you toward mutual understanding and achievement of common goals. What sets consultative professionals apart from others is their ability to manage interactions with clients like turning lights on in a dark room. These professionals take it step by step. They learn from observing both the other person's and their own reactions and approaches. Using the framework and techniques in Part Two, you will be able to prepare a plan and use flexibility and observation in moving toward a goal.

Part Three presents the third component of The Consultative Approach: the Consultative Process. Today's work processes must be flexible and integrate input from both internal and external customers. Feedback is the driver in determining priorities, concerns, and solutions. The consultative process keeps things moving and builds trust and commitment. Part Three describes in detail the highly effective tools and methodologies that you can use to implement this process.

Part Four consists of a single chapter that consolidates all the skills, tools, and techniques presented throughout the book. The Action Plan itself is a tool that can be applied to any project or other effort to help you attain optimum results.

We conclude with a resources section that lists related books and a glossary of the terms used in this book.

TAKING IT ONE STEP AT A TIME

Learning to work consultatively is like learning to walk. By taking small steps, you and your client can learn moment by moment and ultimately build confidence in each other.

Each section, chapter, model, and exercise in this book is one small step. As you become comfortable with one technique, move on to the next topic, try a new idea, or apply your learning and insights to a more challenging client situation.

Keep in mind that *The Consultative Approach* is designed to be flexible. Adapt it to your own needs. You can serve yourself in no better way than to begin to develop your own consultative approach.

PART ONE

AN EXPANDED TOOLKIT

Almost any new endeavor you undertake—whether it's a sport, hobby, art form, or career—means using a set of tools. In golf, you learn when, where, and how to use the different clubs. Chinese cooking uses different utensils from French or Italian cooking. Oil painting requires different brushes and more supplies than water coloring.

Likewise, in working consultatively you use the tools of communication, observation, openness, insight, and flexibility. The three chapters that follow cover these basic tools and expand upon their importance in working with your clients.

Chapter One discusses what it means to partner with your clients and describes the different roles you may be called on to play as you work consultatively. These roles involve how you work with others and adapt to various situations. At the center of these roles is the role of partner—whatever other role or roles you play, your focus is that of partner. Chapter One also addresses the different types of partnering relationships that occur and describes the factors that make for a successful partnership. Exercises in this chapter will help you assess your current partnering relationships and analyze your current approach to working consultatively to determine where it would be most useful to concentrate your efforts.

Chapter Two introduces the tools of observation and perception. Using these tools, you gain insights and information about your clients and what they care about, which is vital in planning a partnering strategy. In this chapter we provide proven models that will help you capture your observations of others and guide you in developing strategies for working most effectively with them. Chapter Two also addresses the issue of building rapport with your clients, an important aspect of partnering.

In Chapter Three, we discuss the tool of expertise. Obviously, your expertise in your field is a tool you are already well acquainted with. But are you missing opportunities to use your expertise with greater impact? Tools are especially valuable when they can be used in a variety of situations. For example, there's more than one use for a hammer: you can drive or remove nails with it, and you can use it to pry open or close a can of paint. The same is true of expertise.

The more your clients use your expertise, the greater the value and impact you have on the organization. We define *expertise* as the application of information and insights learned from experience. Expertise means not only having technical knowledge in your field but also translating what you have learned from experience and communicating why it is relevant.

Your client's perception of your expertise may also include that of your team, your functional area, or your organization as a whole. Thus, your expertise is demonstrated in the collective capability you represent and the way that helps your clients achieve their business objectives. In Chapter Three we provide you with an expertise tool for powerfully articulating your insights, ideas, and recommendations in a way that demonstrates your value and capabilities.

Once you have mastered these tools, continue on to the later chapters of the book. But begin to use the tools immediately, during client meetings and in more casual conversations, both face to face and on the phone. Think of strategies for how to further use these tools over the long term, in planning and implementing a project or throughout an ongoing relationship with a client.

CHAPTER ONE

WORKING AS A PARTNER

Remember the Consultative Balance graphic from the introduction (Figure 1.1)? The key to keeping the three elements of people, process, and expertise in balance is *partnering:* thinking and behaving collaboratively rather than just providing a service. Working consultatively, as a partner, enables you to produce the best results possible under the circumstances and at the same time develop a mutually beneficial relationship with clients. Partnering is the core role in using a consultative approach.

THE ROLE OF PARTNER

Partnering is multidimensional. Trust, integrity, mutual respect, honesty, open communication, collaboration, and joint accountability and responsibility are essential to working as a partner. Without these attributes, a partnering relationship cannot exist.

In many ways, the role of partner is more a goal than a status you can achieve—more journey than destination—because you must continuously work toward partnership. The better the relationship—the more trust, respect, and open communication you have with your clients, whoever they may be—the more effectively you are using The Consultative Approach.

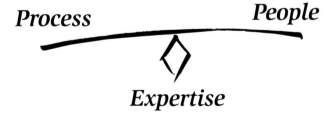

Figure 1.1. The Consultative Balance.

You can be a partner no matter what your task is or how small it seems. Bill Woodson, an expert in family businesses and wealth planning with Arthur Andersen's Center for Family Business, relates this story:

My task was to help a family-owned business agree on a succession plan. They wouldn't listen to me until I recognized that I had to build trust and commitment and develop a partnering relationship with each individual family member—not just the patriarch.

Once I recognized this, I changed my strategy and focused simultaneously on the process, the people, and the advice I knew they needed. I was able to help resolve their individual needs, family difficulties, and business challenges by creating an environment in which we could be partners.

The results were significant, and each family member felt that they had been treated fairly in the process. The family members originally saw me as a financial expert but began to ask for my help in problem solving, facilitating discussions, and coaching them to move toward an agreement. I realized that partnering encompassed both how I worked with them and how they saw me as a business advisor to the family.

THE CONSULTATIVE ROLES

The puzzle in Figure 1.2 shows the roles we have identified as constituting what it means to work consultatively. Notice that the role of partner lies at the center. It's the piece each of the others interlocks with—the core role.

These eight roles are the competencies highly effective people possess in today's changing organizations. In our work, we have found that these professionals are able to adapt to a variety of roles, depending on the particular situation, differences in people's work styles, and the individual personalities involved.

When we ask workshop participants how their clients typically perceive them, they usually identify three roles: (1) technical expert, (2) problem solver (usually in a technical area), and (3) administrator or project manager. By learning to work consultatively, they expand the way they work to include the roles of facilitator, coach, influencer, and strategist. And in integrating all these roles, they are able to partner with clients more effectively. As Laura Penland, vice president at Science Applications International Corporation, explains, "As we move more and more into the Information Age, we are putting technology closer to the end user. As we do that, we have to partner

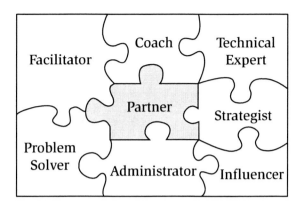

Figure 1.2. The Consultative Roles.

in new ways, play a variety of new roles, and be prepared to meet ever-changing expectations of a variety of client groups."

The distinction between traditional professionals and those who partner successfully is that the latter play a variety of consultative roles, no matter what their job descriptions call for. Because they do so, they are seen as adding critical value. You, too, will notice some changes when clients and organizations begin to perceive you this way. In all likelihood you will begin to receive invitations to meetings from which you were previously excluded. You will probably be asked for your opinion more frequently. And you may receive strategic assignments outside your area of expertise. These are the ways in which clients and organizations demonstrate that they see you as adding value.

We return to the concept of expanded consultative roles in Chapter Three. For now, the most important piece of the puzzle is the Partner piece: the ability to work consultatively.

Your Personal Gap Analysis

The following exercise will help you assess your ability to work consultatively and determine which areas to concentrate on as you progress through this book. You will identify the gaps between how you have worked in the past and how you need to work to function as a more consultative business partner in the future.

The assessment covers three areas: (1) your roles; (2) the people, process, and expertise aspects of the Consultative Balance; and (3) the organizational culture in which you work. You will need to consider each of these areas in terms of the way you have been working and how you need to work in the future. As you complete this assessment, think about the nature of your work and your organization. You'll also need to consider all your clients, internal

Consultative Approach Assessment

What Is in Place	What Needs to Be in Place to Work Consultatively	Closing the Gap
Roles		
What roles have you traditionally played in your job and in your organization?	What is being asked of you in terms of working more consultatively or as a business partner? What behaviors are expected?	What roles or capabilities would be valuable for you to develop in order to close any gap?
List clients with whom you work as a business partner. Describe characteristics of the relationship that enable you to work as a business partner.	What are the areas on which you want to focus in order to work more as a business partner?	Which actions do you need to take with each client?
The Consultative Balance		
What are your capabilities in working with people, using a process, and applying your expertise?	Where are you experiencing the greatest challenges: working with people, using a process, or getting your expertise used?	In which areas would it be valuable for you to develop additional capabilities to close this gap?
People		
What is your attitude toward working consultatively with your clients? How would you evaluate your current skills in working with people in terms of: • Getting buy-in and commitment? • Building relationships?	What challenges are you facing in working with specific clients? Which skills do you feel less than confident about?	In which areas would it be valuable to pay more attention: • Your attitude toward working consultatively? • Your skills and confidence?

Process		
In what ways are your current processes, procedures, and daily routines meeting client needs and expectations?	In what ways are your current processes, procedures, and daily routines *not* meeting client needs and expectations?	What needs to change in how you work with your clients in order to *exceed* their expectations?
In your group or division, are there established operational processes and procedures that are out of date?	Which issues are your clients complaining about that are out of your personal control?	Which operational processes need to be re-examined if you and your group are going to work consultatively?

Expertise		
What are your areas of expertise? What value do you add for your clients?	What expertise do your clients need from you that you are not currently providing?	What skills or knowledge could you develop that would increase your value to your clients?

Organizational Culture		
How would you describe the culture and style of the organization in which you work (for example, collaborative, partnering, forward-thinking, traditional, hierarchical, or somewhere in between)?	What leadership or organizational learning is needed in order to partner with clients and to work consultatively?	What is missing at the leadership and organizational culture level?

or external, at any level in your organization—anyone from whom you need input, support, or commitment. (Types of clients and your interactions with them are discussed in detail in Chapter Two.)

Write down your answers (on a separate sheet of paper) to each of the questions in the Consultative Approach Assessment table. Your answers to the questions in the second and third columns are particularly important—they will tell you what you want to concentrate on and where you most need to apply the ideas in this book.

TYPES OF PARTNERING RELATIONSHIPS

Once an organization or individual determines that partnering is the most effective way of working and that it's worth striving for, it is important to assess the type of partnering relationship desired. Charles Bell, group vice president at Bank of America, describes the approach his organization has taken: "Our overarching strategy is to develop a people culture . . . Our people are our competitive and service advantage. Our business is to manage the human capital at the bank through adding value to performance and helping our business partners to meet their objectives at a lower cost and with higher performance."

Types of partnering relationships vary widely, depending on such attributes as degree of interaction, level of trust, and level of interdependency. To help our clients—organizations and individuals—plan appropriate partnering strategies, we created the model shown in Figure 1.3, which defines partnering categories and their associated attributes. As you review the categories, remember that each of them can be an effective way of working with a client, depending on the client's goals, business issues, in-house resources, budget, and service expectations.

Opportunity-driven partnering is a relationship that meets each party's immediate, self-serving interests. In a personal relationship, this would be the dating stage, or the point at which the parties have not yet developed rapport or chemistry, yet they have enough mutual interest to pursue seeing each other. Organizations and individuals can seek opportunity-driven partnering relationships with clients based solely on basic service needs such as technical expertise.

Transactional partnering relationships have established routines and a contractual exchange as their bases for working together. The relationship is defined by the regular provision of a service and task, such as in a vendor-supplier relationship. Service levels and expectations can easily be defined and measured.

Alliance partnering is characterized by a stronger bond than that of opportunity-driven or transactional relationships. The focus is on the common

Characteristics	Result	
Synergistic • Natural partners • Mutual benefit • In it for the long term • Build commitment	Create new value	**Synergystic**
Alliance • Associate to further common cause • United around the work • Cooperation	Common interests are served	**Alliance**
Transactional • Contractual exchange • Vendor-supplier • Relationship is focused on the task	Provide routine service	**Transactional**
Opportunity-Driven • Opportunity to develop relationship • Serve own best interest • Make sense for now	Meeting self-serving interests	**Opportunity- Driven**

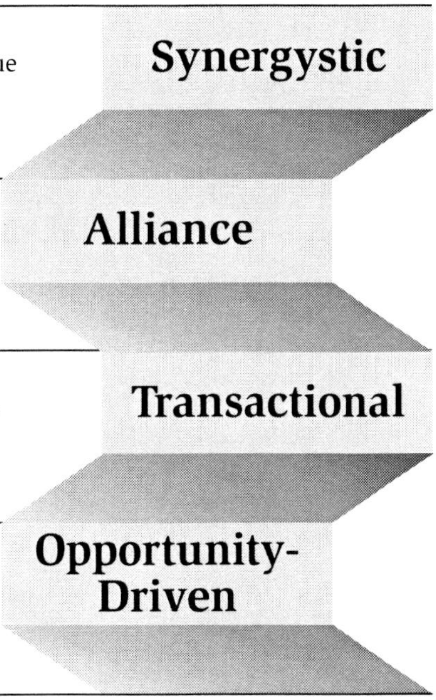

Figure 1.3. Types of Partnering Relationships.

interest of all parties. The association's purpose is to further the cause or goal toward which the parties are working. High-performing self-directed teams work in alliance partnerships, bringing together differing values and approaches and working toward a common goal.

Synergistic partnering relationships are the result of a long-term commitment, and all the parties experience mutual benefit, personal growth, and a willingness to take risks. In this type of partnering the parties challenge ideas, give open and honest feedback, and have the goal of creating new value as a result.

Assessing Your Partnering Relationships

Review the Personal Gap Analysis you completed earlier and think about the types of partnering relationships you have with each of your clients. Does each relationship reflect the type of partnering you desire? Does it allow you to apply your expertise and add value?

To complete this exercise, consider one client relationship at a time and answer each of the following questions on a separate sheet of paper:

1. Where do things stand now? Based on how the client perceives your capabilities, value, and role in the work you do together, which type of partnering relationship best describes your current relationship?

2. Where do you want the relationship to go? Which type of partnering relationship would be best, based on your perception of the client's needs and objectives and your expertise? Are your attitude, knowledge, or skill set helping you or hindering you in your desire to be viewed as a particular type of partner?

3. Which actions can you take to get there? What can you do to move toward the desired type of partnering relationship? Or, if you determine that the current type of partnering is appropriate for the nature of your work together, are there other ways you can demonstrate your value to the client?

As in the previous exercise, your answers to these questions will be useful in determining the use you make of the strategies presented in this book.

PARTNERING COMFORT FACTORS

Think of a situation in which you felt that you were partnering with a client or team member. What was happening? You probably experienced a sense of trust, openness, communication, and caring. Now think of a time in which you felt that you were not partnering with someone. Probably the opposite things were happening: it was hard work; there wasn't a great deal of cooperation; communication and trust were minimal. When you are partnering, both you and your client feel better about the work, the results, and each other.

We have examined different partnering approaches that people use in their work and discovered that six specific factors can be used to assess your level of comfort about partnering.

1. *Common Goals.* Partners share a common goal. Though they may have individual goals, they also have a shared goal—often a higher, overarching goal—that keeps the commitment alive. When goals conflict or are not clearly understood, the ability to partner is jeopardized.

2. *Common Values.* It's very hard for people to feel a sense of partnering if they do not share values. Partners seek to understand what is impor-

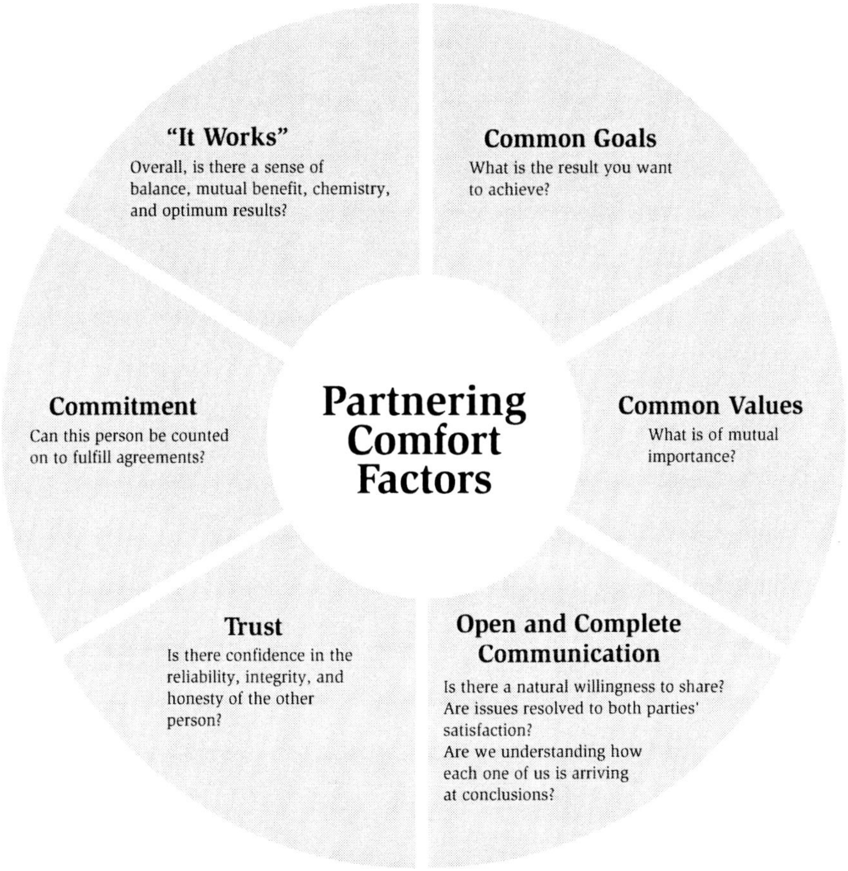

Figure 1.4. Partnering Comfort Factors.

tant to each other and to share a mutual spirit of ethics, appropriateness, valuing of differences, and worldview.

3. *Open and Complete Communication.* Being open with one another can be uncomfortable at times, but it is critical to the survival of the partnership. Openness is speaking one's mind without fear of retribution or judgment, and it enables us to feel complete in our thoughts and actions. Being complete allows us to leave interactions feeling respected by the other person.

4. *Trust.* Trust, which depends on integrity and reliability, is often the deciding factor in determining if one person is comfortable partnering with another. Trust is earned and acquired over time. If trust is lost, so is the partnership.

5. *Commitment.* Successful partners have an attitude of generosity and a willingness to follow through on commitments. They don't keep score. The relationship is not based on a finite benefit but rather on the assumption that giving contributes to growth and prosperity and a "win-win" situation for all involved.

6. *"It Works."* The sixth comfort factor is a gut feeling about the overall partnership and the results you are producing together. Is there a sense of fairness, rapport, mutual benefit, and contribution to the whole? Does the partnership produce an optimum result? "It works" means that both parties have individual strengths and contribute something of value to the relationship as a whole.

The following story illustrates how the comfort factors can help diagnose what is wrong in a working relationship and determine a game plan for improvement.

Our client Dan was struggling with his client Marilyn. She was driving him crazy because they were supposed to be partnering on a large project, and he was worried that they would never make it through the next six months. In evaluating his relationship using the partnering comfort factors, Dan determined that he and Marilyn had the common goal of a successful project. Their values, however, differed.

While both had strong work ethics, Marilyn's approach was, for example, to work all night preparing a report for senior management. And she thought Dan should work through the night with her. Dan also worked hard, but he valued his personal time and he knew that senior management did not read reports immediately. He preferred to strategize and write a quality report rather than work on it through the night.

Dan also felt that Marilyn had a large need for control and expected him to work her way. So Dan did not have a high level of trust with her and was uncomfortable sharing his ideas and feelings.

Once Dan recognized the root of their partnering problems, he decided to take action to limit the effects of their different values. He got agreement on what was a "must have" versus a "nice to have" and developed a work agreement that outlined roles, responsibilities, and the process that Marilyn and he would use in working together. In the end, they achieved their goals, but they agreed that the partnership had been challenging because of their differing values.

Partnering Comfort Factors Assessment

Choose a client that you find it challenging to partner with. Using the definitions of the partnering comfort factors listed earlier and the questions that follow, assess on a scale of 1 to 5 the degree to which each of the factors is present in your relationship with the client.

Review your assessment. What is your overall partnering goal in your relationship? Which comfort factors should you focus on to get closer to your partnering goal?

Now complete this exercise for another challenging client. Are the issues different or similar? If the same issue is problematic for you in other relationships, it probably indicates an area in which you need to build skills. If the issues are different, notice if there are circumstantial factors contributing to the challenges in your relationship.

You may want to refer to this exercise to track the comfort level of your partnering relationships over time or to gauge where you stand as you enter new partnerships.

Partnering Comfort Factors Assessment

Not at All   Sometimes   All the Time

1 -----------2------------3------------4------------5

Partnering Comfort Factor	Client 1	Client 2
Common Goals: Do we both want to achieve the same overall result?		
Common Values: Do we share the same work values?		
Open and Complete Communication: Is there a natural willingness to share? Are issues resolved to both parties' satisfaction? Is there an understanding of how each of us arrives at conclusions?		
Trust: Do I have confidence in the reliability, integrity, and honesty of my client? Does my client have confidence in my reliability, integrity, and honesty?		
Commitment: Can this person be counted on whether things are difficult or going well?		
"It Works": Overall, is there a sense of balance, mutual benefit, positive chemistry, and optimum results?		

CHAPTER HIGHLIGHTS

- Partnering is thinking and behaving collaboratively, not just providing a service.

- The different consultative roles are facilitator, coach, technical expert, strategist, influencer, administrator, problem solver, and, most important, partner.

- Partnering relationships can be divided into four categories: (1) opportunity-driven, (2) transactional, (3) alliance, and (4) synergistic.

- Partner relationships are built on six partnering comfort factors: (1) common goals, (2) common values, (3) open and complete communication, (4) trust, (5) commitment, and (6) an overall sense of "it works."

CHAPTER TWO

GETTING TO KNOW YOUR CLIENTS

Knowing how to work with and influence people is a skill people practice most of their lives, on a daily basis. Yet, when we examined the types of professional challenges people face, working effectively with others always appeared at the top of the list. Managing relationships and finding the best way to work with others requires constant observation, awareness, flexibility, attention to insights and intuition, and adaptability.

Harry Ruffalo, managing partner of Tax, Legal and Business Advisory Services at Arthur Andersen, describes the importance of his client relationships this way: "One of the first things that I learned in my career at Arthur Andersen was to truly get to know the clients I worked with. I would take the time to understand their business, walk the floor, and become one of them. I would always work toward establishing a relationship with the treasurer, CFO, and CEO as well as the tax director."

WHO ARE YOUR CLIENTS?

Before going on, let's redefine what we mean by the term *client*. Simply put, a *client* is anyone with whom you work: those with whom you partner or exchange input, or those from whom you need support or commitment to do your work successfully. That probably covers a broad base of people. Do you have a strategy for partnering with all those client groups? We hope so. This chapter is about reflecting on what you observe during everyday conversations with your clients and using that information to partner more effectively.

A client is anyone who is impacted by your work.

Our first step will be to examine various types of clients and review things to think about in determining how to partner effectively with them. Some of your clients will be involved more than others in your day-to-day activities.

Your challenge is to determine who should be involved and when. Regardless of how often you interact with an individual client or group of clients, it is important to be aware of both their business and personal objectives and their concerns. Knowing their objectives and concerns will help you gain the input, support, and commitment that are critical to your success. This knowledge will alert you to red flags and help to minimize resistance to your project or goal. The following example illustrates how important it is to be aware of all your clients and their individual points of view.

John Lingvall, a performance consultant at Bank of America, told us this story: "I was preparing to facilitate a planning meeting and did not know the people who were attending. Knowing how important it was to find out more about them, I took the senior manager who was sponsoring the meeting out for lunch. I asked him what his objectives were for the meeting and then asked him to describe each of his direct reports (the meeting attendees) one by one. Later I took the time to interview several of his direct reports to get my own sense of them and their perspectives. There were a couple of issues that the senior manager and direct reports didn't see eye-to-eye on. Knowing this prior to the meeting allowed me to strategize on the best approach to take and to run the meeting much more successfully."

CATEGORIES OF CLIENTS

We have found that, generally speaking, clients fall into six categories:

1. Primary
2. Financial
3. Team members
4. Coach
5. Subject matter expert
6. End user

The first three client groups—primary, financial, and team members—will likely have a higher level of involvement in and more direct influence over the process, goals, and outcomes of your work. The other three client groups—coach, subject matter expert, and end users—may have less day-to-day involvement in your work but play key roles at strategic points in the process. These clients can be instrumental to your success in that they provide critical information, perspective, expertise, and support.

Each of the six categories is described in the following sections. As you review them, think about how your own clients fit into these categories and consider which clients have direct or indirect influence over your work. Your challenge is to understand the needs of all client groups and find ways to include them at certain strategic points.

Primary Client

This client is usually your main point of contact for a project or assignment. The primary client provides the direction and scope for the work and often will define your role. This client will interface with others in the organization regarding the work but may not be the final decision maker.

Jean Roux, global strategies and health consultant at Levi Strauss, describes his experience of working with his primary clients: "I have learned that you have to pay special and constant attention to primary clients, no matter how long you have worked with them. Their roles and priorities are constantly changing, so are their commitments and goals. It is critical to ask yourself whether you are still on target with what you are doing and how well you are working together."

When working with your primary client, ask yourself the following questions:

- Does this client know what is involved in this effort for you, for the organization, and for himself or herself?
- Do you have this client's commitment of time and resources?
- How does the client perceive your respective roles?
- Do you share the same vision for the work?

Financial Client

This is the person who authorizes the budget and has final approval over spending priorities. The financial client may or may not be the same as the primary client. If they are not the same, and you do not have access to the financial client, plan with the primary client ways to keep the financial client informed of your work, because that person will probably have concerns about how your project fits with the overall strategic direction of the organization and whether it is a spending priority.

A workshop participant shared the following story about working with a committee of financial clients: "Currently I am working on a cross-functional project team within my company. Our sponsors for the project are two senior managers who really get things done in the organization. Things have been running smoothly up until now. The company has instituted a new policy of reviewing each project's financial picture. So we are writing internal proposals, and our sponsors are presenting them to the funding committee headed by the CFO. Monthly, they review each major project. I have been invited to a few of their meetings to present status reports on our project. While I liked the exposure and experience, it was very intimidating. I had never personally met any of them until then."

When working with a financial client, ask yourself the following questions:

- Who will authorize the budget for this work or assignment?
- Does the client view this effort as an organizational priority?
- What information will this client need, and what is the best way to provide it?
- Could there be other financial clients that I don't know about?

Team Members

Team refers to any group you work with. It could be a project team, a committee, or a task force. Team members can be internal or external to your organization. You must understand each team member's perspective and expectations regarding issues and outcomes.

Michael FitzGerald, executive vice president of CB Commercial Real Estate, stresses the importance of considering each team member as an individual: "We have been moving toward sales and consulting teams as a way to better serve our clients and to differentiate ourselves from the competitor. In doing so, we have to take the time to understand the team members' perspectives and the ways of working most effectively together to define the team's competitive advantage and how to best serve our clients." The net effect, he says, is that this approach enables the team to work "as one" in meeting the client's needs.

When working with a team, ask yourself the following questions:

- What do I need to know about each team member's perspective?
- How can I work most effectively with this group?
- Do team members understand their roles and responsibilities and our collective objectives?

Coach

A coach can help you navigate the political minefield and address your personal concerns about different categories of clients. From this person you can receive invaluable personal feedback, insight, and direction on your partnering strategies. Coaches may be internal or external to your organization. Make sure your coach understands your need for information, support, and feedback.

Kristin Andress, a performance consultant at Arthur Andersen Performance and Learning, describes the value of coaches this way: "At Arthur Andersen Performance and Learning we are reinventing some aspects of how we conduct business and provide services in the future. Not having the luxury to slow down the process, the use of coaches has become key in our ability to respond to our clients. The coach provides objective observations, tools, templates, and techniques on demand. Coaches listen, reflect, and help us strategize."

When working with a coach, ask yourself the following questions:

- What insights can the coach provide on my client groups and on the process I am using with them?
- What feedback can the coach provide on my strategy, approach, and behavior?
- What guidance can the coach provide on relationship building and technical issues?

Subject Matter Expert

A subject matter expert (SME) provides critical information and insights that ensure that the process and solutions are on target. Your SME client may not be dedicated full time to your work together, so think of strategies to maximize his or her effectiveness. Consider which background information you can provide, what input and expertise is needed, and how much involvement you expect from the SME. Because this person is often "invited in," make sure the client feels useful—not used.

Frank Musacchia, a managing director at International Network Services, describes his experience with SMEs: "In our line of business, we work with a variety of subject matter experts, both within our own company and within our vendor companies. Knowing when to involve them and letting them know that their ideas are valuable is critical to getting their support. They take their jobs, ideas, and solutions very seriously and truly want to be useful."

When working with a subject matter expert, ask yourself the following questions:

- At what point in the process do I involve the subject matter expert?
- What role will the subject matter expert play?
- What expectations do I have that I need to communicate?
- How can I ensure that the subject matter expert feels useful and not used?

End Users

End user clients are those whose functions and/or routines are impacted by the results of your project or assignment. They can be internal or external groups and may include your customer's customers. Resistance from end users can be a major hurdle to overcome, so define the end users sooner, rather than later, and involve them in determining issues, solution ideas, and implementation options.

Don Bedford, a program manager at Science Applications International Corporation, told us this story: "We were moving forward on a phone messaging project with a major client. A group of us were discussing the project when one of the team members said, 'I'm just curious—has anyone on this team ever worked the phones to understand our end users' point of view?' The answer was no. At that moment it hit us that taking time to understand the end users' situation was going to be critical to our success."

When working with end user clients, ask yourself the following questions:

- How will this effort impact end users?
- How will I understand the end users' point of view?
- What influences the end users' work environment (for example, culture, norms, constraints, information needs)?
- How will I interface with the end user, and what do I need to discuss?

Insights About Client Categories

Using the following table as a guide, consider each category of client and identify specific individuals you work with who fit into each of the categories. Then, using a separate sheet of paper for each client, list that client's business and personal *objectives* for the project, activity, or assignment you are working on.

Next, write down the client's business and personal *concerns* regarding the project, activity, or assignment.

In reviewing each client's objectives and concerns, did you arrive at any insights you have about the person's situation? Make note of them, taking into consideration the following:

- Why do they have the concerns they do?
- How much stress or pressure are they under?
- What do they need from you?
- What do you need from them?

Client Groups	Business		Personal		Insights About Client
	Objectives	Concerns	Objectives	Concerns	
Primary					
Financial					
Team Members					
Coach					
Subject Matter Expert					
End Users					

LEARNING FROM INTERACTIONS WITH CLIENTS

A key aspect of working consultatively is to partner with all the clients involved in your project or assignment. Knowing their expectations, concerns, needs, and objectives will enable you to develop partnering strategies. Increasing your knowledge about your clients requires making conscious observations during your meetings, phone conversations, and chats in the hallway. Through your ongoing interactions with your clients, you will learn which approaches work and which don't. This will enable you to determine how to improve your interactions in the future.

"If I were to prescribe one process . . . which is fundamental to success in any direction, it would be thorough training in the habit of accurate observation."

—Eugene G. Grace

Every day, you are presented with opportunities to learn more about clients and situations by observing the dynamics of your interactions. We describe this as "using an antennae" to pick up clues from behavior and in the environment. Here is a quick quiz to test whether you use your antennae in making observations.

 Observation Quiz

Recall a recent meeting and try to answer the following questions:

- What were people wearing?
- What were people carrying?
- Did people take notes? If so, what materials were they using?
- If you were in an office, what was on the walls or desk?
- Did the other people drink anything? If so, what was it? Did they use a paper cup? A mug? A glass?
- What were people talking about as they entered the meeting? As they left the meeting?

If you were able to answer most of these questions, congratulations! You used your antennae during the meeting.

Why is it so important to notice the little things? Because it's through observing these subtleties that we gain insights about other people's personality, values, interests, and work style. What you learn from observation will help you build rapport and develop relationships.

Capturing PLOT Observations

Think about past interactions you have had with a particular client. How did he or she behave? Did this client have strong feelings about a particular topic? What was important to this client? What did you learn from the experience? Did you gain any insights that helped you better understand the person?

To work optimally with your clients, you need to run on two tracks during any given interaction. One is the *agenda track:* managing the discussion to reach the desired goal within a specific time frame. The second is the *observation track:* consciously picking up clues about the motivations, concerns, needs, and interests of the other person. Every interaction gives you an opportunity to more deeply understand the other person.

Cliff Pfluger, a messaging analyst at Science Applications International Corporation, told us a story that illustrates the usefulness of observation: "I was recently in a meeting with a client who wanted some new features on the messaging hub. I did not feel that the hub was stabilized enough to add the features and tried to explain that to the client. In a flash, I remembered that this client does not respond to a verbal dialogue but instead loves written diagrams. I quickly drew a system diagram and project plan and explained what we could accomplish by a specific date in order to add his new features. Once he saw it in writing, with dates, steps, and boxes, he immediately understood. Now, when I talk with him I always refer to a written plan."

Staying on the two tracks of managing the discussion and making conscious observations simultaneously requires discipline and focus. We have developed a shorthand tool called PLOT that provides a way to make observations and take quick mental or written notes during interactions.

PLOT is an acronym that stands for *Personality, Language, Opinion/Frame of Reference,* and *Task Approach. Personality* is self-explanatory. How would

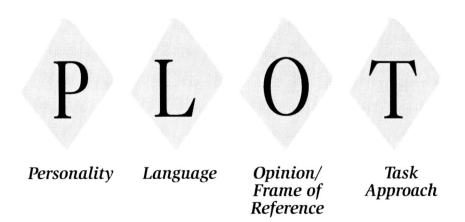

P **L** **O** **T**

Personality   *Language*   *Opinion/ Frame of Reference*   *Task Approach*

PLOT Observation Worksheet

Personality

How would I describe my client's personality?

Language

What body language, tone of voice, and words does my client use?

Opinion/Frame of Reference

What is the client's opinion and frame of reference about the work and about me?

Task Approach

How does my client get things done?

you describe the person to a close friend? *Language* refers to how the person communicates, verbally and nonverbally. *Opinion/Frame of Reference* captures what the person is like to work with in terms of his or her perceptions about you, your work together, and the organization or the world at large. And *Task Approach* describes how this person gets things done.

PLOT is based on methodologies used by salespeople, psychologists, detectives, and consultative professionals who enter a situation, systematically analyze the situation and the people involved, and decide on an appropriate course of action. PLOT can be used either as a mental framework or as a paper-based worksheet. It allows you to capture observations for use either in the moment or in future interactions. You can also share PLOT observations with team members, coaches, and peers as part of feedback, coaching, or strategy sessions. The more you learn about your clients, the more their PLOT thickens!

Practicing PLOT Observations

In this activity, you will progressively complete a PLOT on a client, using the worksheet that follows as a guide. First, think of someone with whom you have had an opportunity to work and consider that person's personal characteristics and working style.

Along with more detailed descriptions of each of the four PLOT elements, samples show how the PLOT tool was used to describe a hypothetical client.

Personality: How would you describe the individual's personality? Examples might be cheerful, aggressive, easygoing, pushy, forceful. (If you are familiar with various personality tools, such as Myers-Briggs, you can use their descriptors here instead.) Having words to describe your client's personality can be helpful when discussing approach strategies with others in coaching situations.

What do your observations of your client's personality tell you about the person? What could you do or stop doing that would improve how you partner with this client?

Personality
How would I describe my client's personality?
• Collaborates if I play by her rules
• Friendly, warm, and personable
• Builds long-term relationships with people
• Motivated by success and balancing work with personal life
• Controlling, but will listen to opinions of others

Language: What body language, tone of voice, and words does the client use? How does your client communicate? In his book *Silent Messages*, Albert Mehrabian shows that body language and tone of voice carry 93 percent of a person's overall communication. What nonverbal clues do you pick up from your client? Is he or she

> *"The most important thing in communication is to hear what isn't being said."*
>
> —Anonymous

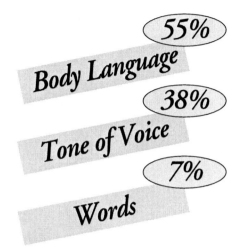

Figure 2.1. How We Communicate.

engaged in or removed from the conversation? Is he or she easily distracted? Does your client's facial expression indicate concerns, resistance, agreement, or commitment? Pay attention to how your client says things. What types of words or phrases does your client emphasize?

Language

What body language, tone of voice, and words does my client use?

- Speaks in vague and general terms
- Uses cheery, upbeat tone of voice
- Writes everything down in calendar or notebook
- Expresses open body language
- Is professional in appearance and manner

 This story comes out of our own experience as consultants: We were preparing to meet a new primary client who had recently replaced someone we had been working closely with for two years. As we had never worked with this person, we were curious and a little anxious about the preconceived notions he may have had about our work and his thoughts about our role in the coming year's strategy. We called him to set the agenda for the upcoming meeting. During the call, his choice of words and tone of voice clearly reflected what was important to him. He repeatedly used the word *flexible:* "We need flexibility," "How flexible are you?" "It has to be modular to allow flexibility," and so on. Every time he used the word *flexible,* his voice became a bit louder and more emphatic. It wasn't exactly rocket science to figure out that flexibility was a top priority for this client. But recognizing the fact enabled us to prepare better for the meeting, and it ended up being the main point of our subsequent discussion.

Think about your specific client again. How would you describe how he or she communicates? What do your observations tell you about the person? What could you do or stop doing that would improve how you communicate with your client?

Opinion/Frame of Reference: What is the person's opinion and frame of reference about the work and about you? Opinion/Frame of Reference refers to how a person sees the world, sees the work, and sees you. Of all the aspects of PLOT, Opinion/Frame of Reference merits the most attention. Lacking information about a client's perspective is like working in a dark room without a flashlight: You just keep bumping into obstacles and can only hope that you are headed in the right direction. By taking the time to find out about your client's opinions and frame of reference you turn on the lights and give yourself full illumination to guide you in your work. By asking questions, observing, and listening, you can capture information and insights about your client's opinions and frame of reference.

The key to finding out about a client's opinions and perceptions is to be curious rather than fearful or defensive. Being open and inquisitive about your client's opinion and frame of reference can help you to uncover hidden biases, concerns, and areas of resistance. With this knowledge and insight, you can plan how to broaden your client's perspective and help to meet his or her needs while avoiding stress for yourself.

If nothing else, focus on understanding your client's opinion and frame of reference.

Similarly, having frequent feedback discussions with your client will let you continue to uncover any unstated or unknown perceptions that could be affecting the work. In turn, the client's horizons will be broadened to consider other options for dealing with challenging situations.

Opinion/Frame of Reference

What is the client's opinion and frame of reference about the work and about me?

- Sees problems as opportunities
- Loves challenges and takes on risks
- Likes to control, wants to confirm long-term strategy of this project
- Is supportive as long as I keep her informed and help her reach objectives
- Hates surprises and is concerned about looking good

We interviewed Mary Jo Potter, managing director of Corporate Alliance, a human resources management consulting company. Among the questions we asked her was how senior management views the notion of partnering. Her response illustrates how observation helps us understand an individual's opinion and frame of reference: "The frame of reference that senior management uses to define partnering is dependent upon their belief and value system. It is usually easy to determine their frame of reference, because what they focus on, pay attention to, and reward should reflect their opinion/frame of reference. What gets confusing is when they talk about one value but act in a contradictory manner. That is when we need to examine more closely their frame of reference and points of view and not take anything for granted."

Think about your specific client again. How would you describe his or her opinion/frame of reference about the work and working with you? Some people are said to view the world "through rose-colored glasses." What color glasses does your client see through? What have you observed about this person in past situations you have had working together? Based on the client's opinion/frame of reference, what are the challenges you face in working with this person? What could you do or stop doing that would improve how you partner with this person?

Task Approach: How does the client get things done? Your client's task approach is easy to observe and provides valuable information. What is the work style of this person: delegator or control freak; detail-oriented or just interested in high-level information? Is this person savvy about company politics and how to get things done in the organization? Is this person respected by others and seen as a team player and a valuable resource? Or is he or she a "mystery employee"—no one can figure out how he or she has kept a job all these years?

Knowing the client's task approach makes it easier for you to think of actions and approaches that match the person's work style. In some situations, you might be able to assist the client in altering his or her task approach for greater efficiency and effectiveness.

Think about your client again. How would you describe his or her task approach? What have you observed in past working situations? How can you make it easy for the client to work with you? What could you do or stop doing that would improve how you partner with this person?

Task Approach

How does my client get things done?

- Considers all options, but usually has one approach she feels strongly about
- Gets to the point ("Okay, tell me what you need.")
- Knows how to work with the company president and CFO to get what she wants and needs
- Rewards and recognizes her staff for their hard work

Observing Levels of Trust

Each aspect of PLOT has a dimension of trust associated with it. How do you know when someone trusts you? Usually you can tell by his or her behavior, by observable clues that give you an indication of how much the person trusts you and your capabilities. Partnering requires a high level of trust. People must be able to confide in each other openly and not worry about judgments or retribution. An important goal for your client relationships may be to raise the trust level so that you can have more open communication in discussing problems, solutions, concerns, and actions.

Once again, this aspect may not be one that you have consciously observed in your client, but it's likely that you have picked up signals along the way. To help assess trust levels and determine partnering strategies, we have developed a way of identifying your client's trust level based on what you observe during interactions.

Trust Level	Language	Task Approach	Opinion/Frame of Reference
High	Open	Takes Risks	Growth
Medium	Guarded	Hesitates	Safety
Low	Closed	Controls	Survival

Figure 2.2. Levels of Trust.

The chart in Figure 2.2 compares the different levels of trust you can observe by using PLOT. In a high-trust relationship (partnering), the parties communicate openly, are more willing to take risks outside of cultural norms and to utilize creative thinking, and are motivated by growth and contribution to the project's success. At a low trust level, people have more closed or guarded communication, try to control situations and other people, and focus on survival and self-preservation. Assessing your client's trust level allows you to plan ways to increase the degree of openness in the relationship and build toward the growth and mutual benefit that form the basis for partnering.

Trust requires feeling comfortable in being open with another person, telling the truth, and sharing in the ups and downs. Arthur Feather, director of Cisco Systems, expresses it this way: "Building trust is based on honesty, delivering on commitments, and having the right chemistry." Some clients may take "baby steps" in moving up to a higher trust level, while others may move naturally into high trust mode. Certain circumstances—such as working intensely on a project, solving a mutual problem, or celebrating a success—can influence your collective abilities to develop a high level of trust. High-risk situations also can accelerate the building of trust. Strong trust leads to better results and much more enjoyable work.

> "Everyone is trying to accomplish something big, not realizing that life is made up of little things."
>
> —Frank A. Clark

It is also important to realize that your own trust level is an important part of the partnering equation. It is difficult to mask low trust, so if your trust level is low, your client probably senses it in how you interact. Often, operating at a higher level of trust will trigger the same response in the other party. In other words, trust creates trust. And once high trust has been achieved, it can be sustained with quality interactions.

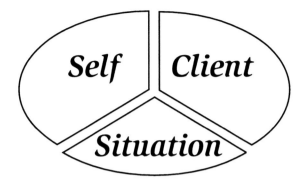

Figure 2.3. Focus on Self, Client, and Interaction.

Consider again the client you were thinking about in the previous exercise. Where do you think the trust level is in the relationship? What behaviors have you observed that give you that indication? What actions can you take to raise the trust to a higher level? What concerns do you have about building trust and commitment with this client?

Seeing Three-Dimensionally

In any interaction, to partner effectively, you must "see" in three dimensions. That is, there are three important areas on which you must focus simultaneously: (1) your own thoughts and reactions; (2) the client's body language, tone of voice, and words; and (3) the general situation—the purpose of your discussion, potential outcomes, and environmental factors. These three "dimensions," like the three visual dimensions of height, width, and depth in the physical world, supply the information you need to move around safely and effectively. Being conscious of yourself, the client, and the situation during an interaction enables you to stay engaged in the conversation while learning new insights you can apply in the future.

A participant in one of our workshops told the following story about the challenge of remaining focused on each of these dimensions: "I was conducting a review for an employee who had been working on a team assignment for a year. He told me in an emphatic tone of voice that he was expecting a promotion to the next grade level as a result of his hard work. I knew that the conversation was not going to be easy, since I did not share his opinion. As we continued, he became more and more emotional, and I became very defensive. The rest of the discussion was totally unproductive. In addition, he kept getting beeped and felt obligated to return the message. To be honest, I was glad about the interruption, since I needed to collect my thoughts. As a manager, I have a hard time when people get upset with me, particularly when I've made a decision that disappoints them."

The challenge in many interactions is twofold, as the story illustrates: You must trust your emotions, concerns, and reactions (positive or negative). But you must also avoid letting your feelings get in the way of staying focused, listening to the client, and assessing the appropriate response. Working consultatively requires that you progress toward your goals (both short-term and long-term) while simultaneously building trust and commitment.

Observing Your Interactions

For one day, pay close attention to your interactions. Determine whether they are positive or negative experiences for you and for the client and whether there is an overall feeling of moving the situation forward. Use the table format and the steps that follow to capture your observations.

Positive and Negative Experiences

List of Interactions	Self (+/−)	Client (+/−)	Situation (+/−)

1. List each interaction in the first column.

2. Evaluate whether the interaction listed was a positive or negative experience for you, the client, and in moving the situation forward and place a (+) or (−) in the appropriate column.

3. In reviewing the positive situations, what actions did you take that contributed to the success of the interaction? In interactions for which you have more minuses, what did you observe about yourself or the other person that made you feel that way?

4. Consider whether there are any observable patterns or conclusions that can be drawn concerning your actions, your clients' behavior, or certain types of situations.

BUILDING RAPPORT WITH CLIENTS

Building rapport is an important aspect of partnering that must be nurtured in order to thrive. Rapport can be threatened or broken during the course of conversations by distractions and other factors: time pressures, lack of focus, ignoring behavioral clues. Don't minimize the negative impact these factors can have on an essential part of your client relationship!

Good rapport is about feeling a connection with the other person and knowing that there is a certain natural flow to the conversation. This connection is the basis for developing partnering and trust. When rapport is in place, there is a sense of mutual respect and an opportunity to influence each other's thinking and way of behaving.

From the client's point of view, when there is rapport the client usually feels that

- You understand the client's world and his or her reality

- You respect and appreciate the client and his or her work

- You are speaking the client's language and are on the same wavelength

---

Tod Grantham, managing director at International Network Services, stresses the necessity of building rapport: "I interview many consultant job candidates. One characteristic I look for is the ability to recognize the need to build rapport with clients. During the interview process, I ask consultant candidates to respond to the following situation: 'It is your first day on a new project with a new client. You enter a conference room for the project initiation meeting and find the client manager responsible for hiring us seated at a table, flanked by two other staff members who appear agitated. You learn from the ensuing discussion that International Network Services has been retained to help the client meet a project deadline. The project is already six months into a one-year duration, but it is nowhere near 50 percent complete. There is a distinct difference of opinions between the client manager and the staff members. The staff members are openly hostile toward you, the INS account team, and their own management throughout the meeting. You know that you must gain the complete cooperation of these individuals regarding project and environmental specifics, or you will not be able to avail them of your expertise in time to meet the project deadline.' Then I ask the candidate: 'Given these parameters, how do you initiate this project?'

"The range of answers to this question is sometimes astounding. I know I have found a potential employee when the response contains two key elements. First, the recognition that rapport must be established and barriers addressed before any progress can be made and, second, the understanding that the consultant must position himself or herself as an experienced but nonthreatening peer-level resource whose sole purpose is to empower the client's staff to succeed.

"Understanding when and how to develop rapport seems like common sense, but for many people it does not come naturally, and as a result they miss opportunities to develop partnerships with clients."

Mirroring and Matching

One subtle way to build rapport is to align yourself physically with the client's "frame of reference"—to mirror his or her behavior. *Mirroring and matching* means using your own body language, tone of voice, and words to reflect the body language, tone, and words used by the other person. This might include matching your client's posture or the pace and vocabulary he or she uses when speaking.

To be effective, mirroring and matching must be accomplished in a natural manner. In fact, in using the observation skills you have been practic-

"To act like one is to be one."

—Lao Tzu

ing, you may have noticed yourself or your clients unconsciously mirroring and matching others. It's one of many behaviors human beings (and other primates) normally use to reassure each other that they are not threatening. Used well, mirroring and matching create a comfort zone and a feeling of connection.

Joyce Bennett, a total quality manager at United Defense, related an interesting example of using mirroring and matching with a client. Joyce and her team went to greater lengths than you may ever need to, but this story illustrates how the technique can be useful in a difficult situation. "After a recent merger, I was assigned to assist a plant in developing a new culture. The colonel in charge was a West Point graduate who had spent his military career overseeing the building of fighting vehicles for the Army. The first thing my team and I decided was that we would wear Army-green suits and stand at parade rest when we were meeting with the colonel. As funny as this may sound, the minute he saw us he began to relax.

"We learned how to talk to him. During the first week we worked with him, he kept asking, 'How will we make sure the troops are happy?' We immediately began calling the employees the troops, and he felt understood. This was the beginning of a long and successful partnership."

Building Rapport and Observation Practice

Use the following suggestions to practice your observation, rapport building, and mirroring and matching skills.

• Pay attention to situations in which rapport is immediate. Notice how you are unconsciously mirroring the other person. Are you sitting in a similar position? Do you choose similar words or a similar tone of voice to express yourself? In a conversation with someone where rapport seems to be inadequate or lacking, notice the other person's posture and any gestures he or she might be using, then mirror them. If the person leans forward, you lean forward. If the person crosses his or her legs, cross yours. Notice whether this technique leads to an increased sense of rapport.

• Practice changing the volume, speed, or pitch of your voice to match that of the person to whom you are speaking. You don't need to mirror his or her exact tone, but you need to be close. (Note that this may not be advisable in situations that are tense or angry. Mirroring someone who is shouting, for example, will probably lead to more shouting, not rapport.)

• Listen for key words that the client repeats. How does the client refer to employees, staff people, associates, team members, workers? Use the same words in response.

- How does the client express himself or herself? In descriptive, colorful stories; with technical language or jargon; using short, plain words or an erudite, multisyllabic vocabulary? The client will probably feel both greater rapport and more respect for you if you respond in a way that matches how he or she thinks.

Mirroring and matching often feel awkward in the beginning. You will become more comfortable with these techniques as you integrate them into your own natural style.

CHAPTER HIGHLIGHTS

- List your clients by client category: primary, financial, team members, coach, end users, and subject matter experts. Consider each client's business and personal objectives and concerns.
- Develop strategies for when and how to involve clients from each client group for input and buy-in along the way—not just at the beginning and end of your work.
- Develop a PLOT on your clients as a regular way of working. Use the PLOT information to plan your partnering strategies and receive coaching from others.
- Determine the level of trust in your relationship with your clients as part of your PLOT observations. Look for ways to work at higher levels of trust with individuals and groups.
- Work toward building rapport with your clients by observing interactions closely (including your own reactions) and mirroring and matching your clients' body language and speech patterns.

CHAPTER THREE

PROVIDING VALUE
BEYOND KNOWLEDGE

Expertise is a commodity that your clients and organization expect you to provide. Traditionally, in the role of "expert" you supplied primarily critical technical knowledge; that is, information about your particular area of expertise. But more may be expected of you now. Are you asked to make linkages between what you know as an expert and the strategies, concerns, and problems your clients face? Are you playing a broader and more visible role in the achievement of your organization's and your clients' business goals?

Our experience with client organizations shows that understanding the client's business, proactively addressing the needs of internal and external clients, and influencing how change is managed and solutions are implemented are all part of the expanded role of today's "expert." The approach offered in this chapter will help guide you toward becoming more than a technical expert—to becoming a true business partner able to provide value beyond knowledge.

> *"Life is like playing a violin solo in public and learning the instrument as one goes on."*
>
> —Samuel Butler

WHAT IS EXPERTISE?

The seventh edition of *Webster's New Collegiate Dictionary* defines *expertise* as "an expert opinion or know how." Expertise can be observed by others, and people usually have a sense of who possesses "know how" and who doesn't. In your work it is probably important to be seen as an expert, but are some aspects of your "know how" going unseen and unappreciated?

A friend recounted to us the following story of an early experience of being an expert: "I once won an award in a spelling bee at school. I didn't have very many friends, so the attention from my teacher and class meant a lot. I felt smart and important. My prize was a blue ribbon, which I still have to this day. What my classmates saw during the contest was my ability to spell difficult words. What was invisible was the method I had taught myself to become a master speller. After the contest, my teacher had me explain my method to the class. I was more popular after that."

As this story illustrates, while technical skill or knowledge is important, personal insights, methodologies, and learnings are also valuable—perhaps even more so.

For the purposes of The Consultative Approach, we have broadened Webster's definition, interpreting *expertise* as "the application of information and insights learned from experience." Information is gathering "know how" and being an "expert in something." Insights are your life's learnings or "internal knowledge" gained from experience. Your insight is very valuable to your clients, to your employer, and to your co-workers. You probably have plenty of ideas that can help someone make a better decision, avoid going down the wrong path, implement a program more successfully, or simply sleep better at night. The application part is how you get across your knowledge and insights to clients. Unfortunately, in some cases the very nature of your role or type of work can limit how people perceive your value, as the following story illustrates.

The speaker here is a client of ours, an expert in recruiting, who faces challenges in sharing her insights to show her value. "As a recruitment manager in human resources, my responsibility is to work with the line managers to help them locate and hire the right people. Unfortunately, most of the managers don't know enough about what I do to really use my capabilities well, so I spend a lot of time training them. They treat me like an order taker and don't want to listen to my ideas on how to best fill the open positions.

"There is one manager, however, who invites me in during her strategic planning sessions to discuss staffing issues. She has gained a much deeper understanding of what I do, and as a result I am better able to meet her staffing needs and hire more qualified people for her. If only I could get all the other managers I support to involve me in this way."

Working consultatively enables you to make the invisible aspects of your expertise visible to your clients. You do this by sharing your insights in ways that meet the client's needs. Simply put, most clients are worried about two things:

1. Meeting their business objectives
2. Overcoming concerns they have about meeting their business objectives

If you have ideas and recommendations for addressing those areas, your clients will be mesmerized. If your expertise is shown by providing information only, the burden is on the listener to search for relevance. If the listener isn't interested—because the information seems extraneous—he or she will probably get lost or distracted. But when you share insights relevant to the client's situation, he or she is much more likely to listen to and be engaged in what you have to say.

Ask yourself two things:

1. What are the issues this client is most worried about?
2. How can my expertise address those issues?

Answering these two questions means that you connect what you know to why it would be meaningful to the listener. And that's a good beginning.

Then you must present that information to the client in such a way that he or she can quickly understand and immediately see the value of your expertise. It includes talking from your head and your heart, sharing your life's learning and passion for your field of knowledge, and demonstrating genuine concerns for the client's best interest: meeting their objectives and addressing their concerns.

Jeffrey Totten, director of tax education at Arthur Andersen, illustrates this point: "It used to be that tax professionals were applauded if they could repeat a tax code off the top of their heads. A professional who provided information in this way today would be perceived as unable to communicate with the average person . . . and the average person is our client."

Let's summarize these concepts. Your expertise has dimensions beyond your know how. In working consultatively, expertise includes all of the following:

- Information and insights learned from experience
- Knowledge about business issues
- Skill in making the invisible visible

- Messages from the heart and the head
- Connection with what is important to the listener
- Ability to draw on life's learnings and your passion
- Demonstration that you understand the client's objectives and concerns

MAKING EXPERTISE STATEMENTS

Most of the time, when you share your expertise, it is done on the spur of the moment—without much time for preparation. Even in these impromptu exchanges it is important to articulate clearly your opinions and recommendations, to tap into your experience base, and to share information and insights that relate to and impact the client. But doing this clearly and concisely is not always easy.

The Expertise Statement Model

We developed the following graphic model to illustrate how to make an Expertise Statement that connects your experience with what is of interest to the client. This communication tool is designed to help you organize your thoughts, clearly articulate your insights, and make a powerful impact.

The three parts of the Expertise Statement Model flow from what you have learned from experience and build a bridge to the listener's needs and interests. The Experience Statement ("What my experience has been") establishes your credibility. The Findings Statement ("What I learned from that experience") is the insight or learning gained from the experience. The Relevance Statement ("How what I learned applies to now") is the connection to the current situation, objectives, or concerns. These components combine to form a powerful and compelling message to your client: your Expertise Statement. Before we give examples of this model in action, consider the following important tips:

- *Consider the listener's perspective.* Before making an Expertise Statement, think about the client's perspective. Consider the context of the conversation, the person's point of view, and level of acceptance or resistance to the situation and to you. How can you draw on your past experiences in discussing this person's objectives and concerns?
- *Use a hook to engage the listener.* What is the client most interested in? Probably something related to achieving objectives or addressing concerns. What will draw the listener into wanting to continue the conversation?

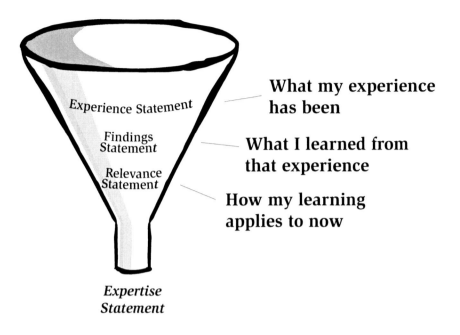

Figure 3.1. The Expertise Statement Model.

The best hooks use your experience of a positive or negative consequence related to the client's situation: saving time or money, increasing sales, reducing overhead, increasing costs, and good or bad publicity are all attention getters.

• *Be succinct.* Make sure your Expertise Statement is concise and gets to the point quickly. Remember that most people have a limited attention span to start with. Add in typical workplace distractions, and keeping someone focused on what you are saying can be very challenging. Brevity makes what you say much more memorable.

• *Use "we" statements.* Statements that use the word *we* subtly suggest that you are a team player. Broadly speaking, *we* could refer to the experiences of your group, team, or company that might be of value to a client. *We* can also include the client to whom you are speaking.

The following are some examples of Expertise Statements used by participants in our workshops to influence their clients. Phrases shown in italics are the hook.

Getting the Client's Time

Janet complained that her client Bill was resistant to meeting with her as often as she would like. She needed him to be up-to-date and involved, in case she ran into obstacles. Knowing that he was concerned about the success of the project, she used the following Expertise Statement to influence his thinking about setting up a regular meeting:

Experience: "In working on projects like this one . . . "

Findings: " . . . I have found it critical to our success to keep my client regularly informed of our status *so that as issues arise, or if we run into problems, we can address them immediately.*"

Relevance: "Based on our short time table for completion and little room for rework, I suggest that we set aside thirty minutes each week for update meetings. That way we will always be on track."

The hook in this example suggests that the project may have problems that require a quick response from the client.

Getting Buy-in and Budget

The consultant in this next situation is a systems engineer working with an internal client on the installation of computer workstations at a variety of sites. The consultant wanted the client to agree to setting up a preinstallation testing area as a norm for all future installations. Here is what he said:

Experience: "Our experience with the recent customer fulfillment center provided some key lessons."

Findings: "Since we did not create a preinstallation testing area, we were unable to test the system ahead of time. *When the customers experienced problems, we were unable to respond intelligently, and we all became highly frustrated.*"

Relevance: "In the future we can *reduce the installation time by 50 percent and maintain customer satisfaction* if we design a preinstallation testing area for new sites."

This Expertise Statement engaged the client so well that the conversation led to an immediate action plan and budget allocation for creating a preinstallation testing area.

In the next several meetings you attend, listen as people share their expertise. Do they make a negative or positive impact on you? What do they do that is effective or ineffective? Do you hear a hook?

Taking into account the other person's perspective, engaging the listener with a hook, and being succinct will make major differences in whether or not people listen to your ideas. Also be sensitive to the fact that people may not want to know everything you know about a topic. They do, however, want to know of your information and insights that are relevant to their situation, as the following story illustrates:

One day a little girl came home from school ready to begin to work on a school report about Argentina. She approached her mother to ask a question about the country and the people who lived there. Her mother turned to her and suggested, "Why don't you wait and ask your father when he gets home?"

The little girl responded, "Okay, but you know how he is, and I don't need to know that much about it!"

Practicing Expertise Statements

To get started making Expertise Statements, think of a situation in which you might have the opportunity to share your expertise or influence a client in a specific direction. Take a few minutes to write an Expertise Statement. Be sure to include statements that establish your credibility, relate what you have learned or observed from your experience, and describe how that relates to the client's objectives or concerns.

When you have finished, ask a co-worker or friend to listen to your Expertise Statement and give you feedback. It would be helpful if the listener knew the client and the situation, but it is not critical.

Continue practicing with making Expertise Statements until you get comfortable, and they feel spontaneous.

EXPANDING YOUR EXPERTISE

While your technical expertise is your calling card that gets you in the door in today's work world, it is not enough. People will assume that you have the technical expertise necessary to do your job. However, as mentioned in Chapter One, they will also expect that you can search for solutions, influence thinking, and facilitate decision making and commitment. In addition, you will be expected to align your work with strategic business plans and be able to build partnerships with people. We refer to these expanded work capabilities as the Consultative Roles that are required to work as a business partner.

Revisiting the Consultative Roles

These Consultative Roles take into consideration the Consultative Balance of effectively working with people, managing a collaborative process, and applying your expertise to demonstrate the range of your capabilities.

The eight Consultative Roles function as follows:

1. The *Technical Expert* gives information and advice.
2. The *Strategist* develops the game plan and overall direction.
3. The *Influencer* sells ideas, broadens perspectives, and negotiates.
4. The *Administrator* manages schedule, budget, and resources.
5. The *Problem Solver* searches for clues and evaluates solutions or provides a process to solve problems.
6. The *Facilitator* keeps the process moving and on track.
7. The *Coach* provides motivation and feedback and helps develop others.
8. The *Partner* balances results with client trust and commitment though collaboration.

Traditionally, what roles have you played in your work? Technical Expert? Administrator? Problem Solver? Are you finding that your clients want you

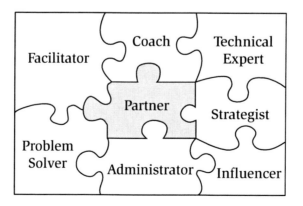

Figure 3.2. The Consultative Roles.

to do more? If so, look for ways to expand your expertise beyond your habitual modes. Focus on developing one or more of these roles so that you will be ready to respond when the opportunity arises.

Preston is a performance consultant for a large high-tech company. He told us the following story about how the range of Consultative Roles helped him. (The specific roles that he used are shown in brackets following the examples of their use.) "I was recently meeting with Jennifer, a division manager of my company, and Joe, her special projects person. Our purpose was to discuss the overall game plan for a sales training project that Joe and I would be working on together. Both clients saw me as a training expert [Technical Expert] and interested in helping with their training needs [Problem Solver].

"We were discussing a strategy for implementing a series of workshops [Strategist], when Joe launched into a litany of questions about administrative details related to resources, budget, and time. I switched direction and focused on discussing implementation details [Administrator] based on the limited information I had at that moment. I then directed the conversation back [Facilitator] to the overall strategy for the sales training. Jennifer mentioned that some of the sales managers had not been happy in the past with some of our training. I asked her questions to find out what the real issues were and suggested that I contact the sales managers directly to get more information [Problem Solver]."

From this example, you can see the variety of roles that Preston played in just one interaction. If he had stayed only in the role of technical expert or problem solver, his ability to partner with the client would have been diminished. The key to using the roles is to navigate from one Consultative Role to another based on the demands of the situation. This is another example of using your expertise in the moment.

If switching roles in this manner seems like too much of a stretch, and you have resources available, think about bringing in other team members to play specific roles. This way, the client will see you as both understanding what is needed and exceeding their expectations. The exercise that follows will help you determine specific actions you can take to expand the roles you play in working with your clients.

Consultative Roles Assessment

This tool was developed to give you a more in-depth look at each of the Consultative Roles and, based on your assessment, to consider actions you can take to improve in each.

To complete the assessment, think of a client with whom you would like to develop more of an overall partnering relationship. For each question, consider how important the specific behavior is to the client and then how often you apply the behavior. It is best to rate first the importance for all the items for a given role and then go back and rate how frequently you apply the behavior. Use a scale of 1 to 5: 1 if the behavior is not at all important or applied; 5 if the behavior is important or applied all the time.

After you have completed the two columns, add up each of them and enter the totals in the spaces provided. Then subtract the Importance total from the Apply total, and enter the result on the Gap line. If the gap is a negative number it means that you don't apply that consultative role as often as you perceive it is needed.

Example:

Facilitator

	Import	Apply
1. Manage discussions effectively	5	3
2. Demonstrate flexibility	5	5
3. Ensure that everyone understands the steps we will follow in working together	3	4
4. Focus on making sure that others are in agreement before moving on	2	5
5. Move the project or assignment along	5	2
Total	20	19
GAP		−1

Facilitator

	Import	Apply
1. Manage discussions effectively		
2. Demonstrate flexibility		
3. Ensure that everyone understands the steps we will follow in working together		
4. Focus on making sure that others are in agreement before moving on		
5. Move the project or assignment along		
Total		
GAP		_____

Problem Solver

	Import	Apply
6. Take the time to analyze and thoroughly understand the needs of the project, task, or assignment		
7. Proactive in recognizing potential problems		
8. Involve others in identifying and solving problems		
9. Develop a process or plan to solve problems		
10. Explore several options for solutions		
Total		
GAP	_____	

Coach

	Import	Apply
11. Know what motivates others		
12. Ask for ideas on how to work effectively with others		
13. Aware of own personal reactions to a situation before responding		
14. Help others in developing knowledge and skills		
15. Provide and ask for feedback		
Total		
GAP	_____	

Technical Expert

	Import	Apply
16. Competent in developing solutions and formulating recommendations		
17. Relate technical or complex information so that it is valuable to others		
18. Encourage people to hear and "buy in" to ideas		
19. Appreciated for specific knowledge and skills; viewed as a valuable resource		
20. Respected for technical capabilities		
Total		
GAP	_____	

Administrator

	Import	Apply
21. Provide those involved in a project or assignment with a written summary of roles, responsibilities, and resources required		
22. Understand the policies and procedures for utilizing resources		
23. Provide project status		
24. Manage the budget efficiently		
25. Demonstrate the ability to manage time and deadlines		
Total		
GAP	_____	

Influencer

	Import	Apply
26. Recommendations are usually acted upon		
27. Able to persuade when faced with a differing opinion		
28. Present options and trade-offs		
29. Able to obtain what is needed to do the job		
30. Focus on a win-win experience during a negotiation		
Total		
GAP		_____

Stategist

	Import	Apply
31. Make sure the big picture is considered		
32. Strategically involve key stakeholders in the process		
33. Create a game plan for achieving the best results in working together		
34. Understand client's business, strategies, and needs		
35. Understand client's objectives and concerns		
Total		
GAP		_____

Partner

	Import	Apply
36. Create a high level of trust and commitment in working relationship		
37. Regularly determine whether expectations are being met		
38. Ensure that there is a common goal toward which we are both working		
39. Establish open communication as a cornerstone of the relationship		
40. Develop a sense of partnership		
Total		
GAP		_____

You can also use this assessment with your clients. Ask them to rate you on the behaviors listed, then compare your rating to theirs and discuss what you should be doing more of and less of to further develop the relationship. Participants in our workshops have found this to be an extremely valuable strategy and a way to initiate a discussion on true partnering.

CHAPTER HIGHLIGHTS

- *Expertise* is the application of information and insights learned from experience.

- Expertise is more than playing the role of technical expert and problem solver. It is playing all of the Consultative Roles, including facilitator, coach, administrator, strategist, influencer, and partner.

- Making Expertise Statements ties what you have learned from experience to the listener's needs and interests. It includes what your experience has been, what you learned or observed, and how that insight relates to a client's situation.

- In using Expertise Statements, remember to do the following:
  - Consider the listener's perspective.
  - Use a hook to engage the listener.
  - Be succinct.
  - Use "we" statements.

PART TWO

THE ART OF MANAGING CLIENT INTERACTIONS

Before we begin, let's consider some examples of challenging client interactions.

Chris, a network engineer, was talking with his client, Bob, about a problem. Bob had become agitated: his voice was loud, his face was red, and he looked ready to explode as he said, "Chris, just what is the problem here?" Chris's tone matched Bob's as he gave a very technical response and tried his best to convince his client that he would take care of the situation. But the more he talked, the more upset they both became.

Lynda, a performance consultant, had been working on a project to define job competencies for a client group. The previous meetings had gone well, and Lynda felt that the project was moving at a good pace. She was ready to present the competencies for two of the five groups. Then, at 5 P.M. one day, Lynda got a phone call from Michelle, her primary client, asking her to present the competencies for all five groups the next afternoon. As Lynda listened, all she could think was "I only have information on two groups. I'm not prepared to talk about all five groups!" She struggled to convince Michelle to delay the presentation.

Did these situations sound familiar to you? Challenging and potentially sensitive client interactions such as these can—and do—happen every day. They can happen at any point in a project. They are the moments in which you must think on your feet and be flexible in order to turn acrimony, confusion, or unreasonable requests into situations that build trust and move the client relationship forward. We focus on these types of challenging interactions in the next three chapters. The quality of the interaction is the most important concern in managing client interactions. We focus on both planned and spontaneous interactions as the in-the-moment opportunities that enable you to impact, influence, and add value—whether you are in the boardroom or the back room.

Consciously managing client interactions and staying in the moment provide the opportunity to employ all the consultative roles: partner, strategist, problem solver, facilitator, coach, influencer, technical expert, and administrator. While some interactions, such as presentations or meetings, may be more formal than others, remember that all of them require the ability to make decisions and to target your responses on the spot to produce optimum results and build trust and commitment. Let's see what Chris and Lynda had to say about their client interactions.

"We do not remember days, we remember moments."

—Cesare Pavese

"Bob was defensive," Chris said. "As a result, I became defensive and was unable to make my point—that we could have a bigger problem on our hands than the one Bob was worried about. Besides, I had another meeting I had to go to, and I was running late."

Lynda had this to say: "I was so caught off guard by her request that I didn't know exactly how to respond. I felt like I was between a rock and a hard place."

Both Chris and Lynda had difficulty working consultatively in the moment. Each interaction resulted in a lost opportunity to better understand what the client needed and to identify mutually beneficial solutions.

THE MANAGING CLIENT INTERACTIONS MODEL

In Part One you practiced thinking as a partner, observing your own and your clients' reactions and situational factors, and presenting your expertise (information and insights) in ways relevant to your client's needs. Now, building on those skills, it's time to learn the art of managing each stage of your client interactions. To assist you, we have developed the following interaction tool, which models an approach to managing interactions. The result is a positive experience for you and your client and an overall sense of partnering and trust.

The main steps of the Managing Client Interactions Model are as follows:

- Get ready for the interaction by focusing in the moment and minimizing distractions.
- Define a goal to guide you during the conversation.
- Question to understand the person's opinion/frame of reference and situation.
- Listen for ways to partner and build rapport through observing body language, tone of voice, and words.
- Refine your goal for the interaction if necessary based on what you are learning about the client's opinion/frame of reference and situation.
- Respond from a partnering point of view, using observations and considering the consultative roles that might be useful in this interaction.

Because interactions by nature are cyclical, so is the Managing Client Interactions Model. The arrow that connects *Respond* to *Question* indicates that you are managing the dynamic flow of information and insights during the exchange.

In the three chapters that follow, we walk through the steps of the Managing Client Interactions Model and the techniques associated with each. Chapter Four covers the two initial steps: getting ready and defining your goal for the interaction. Chapter Five discusses the important information-gathering steps of the model, what we call peeling the onion: questioning and listening. Chapter Six concludes the model with the last two steps: refining your goal for the interaction and responding to the client.

Any art form—whether it's painting or dance or writing—requires practice and attention to detail. Managing client interactions effectively is no different. It requires thinking and acting consciously, using different and new

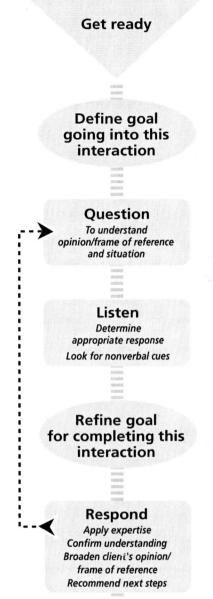

Get ready

Define goal going into this interaction

Question
To understand opinion/frame of reference and situation

Listen
Determine appropriate response
Look for nonverbal cues

Refine goal for completing this interaction

Respond
Apply expertise
Confirm understanding
Broaden client's opinion/ frame of reference
Recommend next steps

techniques and approaches until they become familiar and comfortable. Mastering these skills will prove invaluable to you over time, and it is altogether likely that you will derive benefits from them even in the learning stages.

CHAPTER FOUR

PREPARING THE CANVAS

We cannot stress enough that managing client interactions is about partnering *in the moment,* using each interaction to move forward the levels of trust and commitment and the quality of results. Two elements are key to managing client interactions successfully: (1) you must get ready by putting yourself in a partnering frame of mind; then (2) you must focus on playing the consultative role of facilitator to keep the dialogue open and moving forward to complete resolution. In order to do the latter, you must have a goal in mind for the current interaction—what you want to accomplish during this conversation.

Getting focused and defining your immediate goal are the topics covered in this chapter. Together, they can be considered equivalent to the work an artist does in preparing to paint: applying a base coat to the canvas and sketching the outlines of what she wants to render.

Managing client interactions is partnering with others in the moment.

GET READY

The first stage of any client interaction is to get ready mentally and physically. It doesn't matter whether you are preparing for an informal meeting or a major presentation—this is an important stage. This first stage can be subdivided into two parts:

1. Putting yourself in a partnering frame of mind in order to stay present and focused in the moment

2. Minimizing distractions

You've already learned what it means to be in a partnering frame of mind. Remember the three areas of focus we discussed in Chapter Two? During client interactions, you need to focus simultaneously on your own thoughts

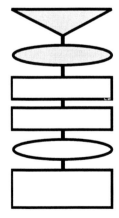

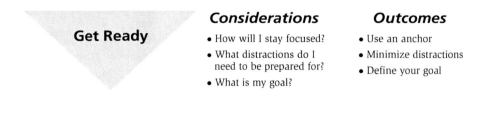

Get Ready	*Considerations*	*Outcomes*
	• How will I stay focused?	• Use an anchor
	• What distractions do I need to be prepared for?	• Minimize distractions
	• What is my goal?	• Define your goal

and reactions; the client's body language, tone of voice, and words; and the general situation—the purpose of your discussion, potential outcomes, and environmental factors. Together, these make up what might be called a partnering awareness. Being conscious of these three elements enables you to stay engaged in the conversation while learning from the interaction in ways that you can apply in the future.

This story, told to us by Catherine Card, a distributed support and operations consultant at Science Applications International Corporation, illustrates the challenge of maintaining a partnering focus—making a conscious choice to respond consultatively in the moment rather than letting survival instincts take over: "I was recently in a meeting with a group of my team members and clients. One team member challenged me, as he was concerned we were going in the wrong direction. Since clients were in the room, my immediate instinct was to strangle the person—or at least ask him if we could talk off-line later! But I caught myself in the moment, took a deep breath, and instead asked him to explain more specifically his concerns with our direction. As he explained, I responded with questions with an emphasis on the client's perspective.

"From that point on, I was able to steer the conversation better and respond to his concerns. By being conscious of not reacting immediately and instinctively but instead exploring the concern, I am able to manage my client interactions like I never could before."

Tips for Focusing

Become a keen observer of what is going on with your client, with yourself, and with the situation. During your interactions, stay focused on the following:

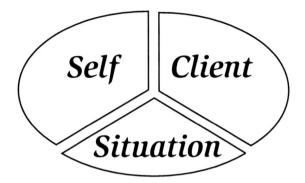

Figure 4.1. Focus on Self, Client, and Situation

- What you are learning about the client's opinion/frame of reference and the strength of his or her feelings and needs
- How you are thinking and feeling, and how you convey your stated and unstated needs
- What is needed to move the situation forward to achieve optimum results

Developing a Partnering Anchor

Getting ready is easy when you have plenty of time to prepare. Given an hour or two to get dressed to go out for the evening, most people turn out looking fairly presentable. But what if a friend calls and says, "I have two tickets to that sold-out show you've been wanting to see. It starts in forty-five minutes. Meet me there." If you're fortunate enough to own a perfect jacket, one that fits great and dresses up whatever you wear it with—and it isn't at the cleaners—you'll be okay. Otherwise, you'll probably arrive either unfashionably late or just plain unfashionable.

What does this have to do with client interactions? Suppose you're at your desk, eating your lunch, and a client you've needed an okay from for several days finally returns your message. He's traveling, calling on a cell phone, and has five minutes between planes. Patience is not his middle name. Suddenly you're on the spot—here's your ticket to the show, so to speak. Do you have a "jacket" to wear?

A "jacket" in this case is what's called an *anchor*—a way of clearing your mind and immediately focusing all your attention on the task at hand. An anchor is something that you do or think that makes you feel good and very "present." It can be as simple as taking a deep breath (and letting it out), thinking a particular word, or snapping your fingers—or it can be more elaborate, when you have the time.

Many people use anchors before performing on stage, competing in sports events, speaking before groups, or conducting sales calls. One client told us that his anchor is to sing along to a tape of his favorite aria while driving to the golf course. The anchor clears his mind and improves his golf game. Other people use visualization, positive affirmations, and relaxation exercises to help them get focused and feeling upbeat before important events.

Coauthor Suzanne Saxe does a dance step as her anchor: "When I first used an anchor, I chose something that would physically and mentally prepare me to sit up and take notice. I remembered how during a jazz class I felt alert, energized, and in tune with myself and the others dancing with me. So I decided to develop a dance step as an anchor that would always remind me of those feelings. I now have a long and short version of my anchor; I choose which one to use depending on the amount of time and privacy I have to get ready. I am amazed at how instantly those positive feelings are re-created."

A partnering anchor will help you establish a collaborative frame of mind before going into an interaction. If you are fearful or anxious going into a situation, these feelings can negatively affect your behavior and concentration, so it is important to enter into a conversation with the most positive, upbeat attitude you can create.

Creating a Partnering Anchor

Anchors should be easy to recall and not take very long to complete. Remember that ideally your anchor will be something you can do anywhere, anytime, to quickly get mentally and physically "present" and focused. You might want to consider the following ideas when developing your own partnering anchor:

- A body movement, such as a dance step, hand gesture, or facial expression

- A sound of some kind such as a song, positive affirmation, tongue twister, or whistle
- A visualization of a positive place or experience
- A relaxation activity, such as breathing slowly and deeply

Jot down your ideas for a partnering anchor. Then pick the one that most appeals to you and try it out for a few days. See whether it helps you prepare mentally and physically to be present and ready for partnering during interactions. If not, change it or try another idea. Have fun creating your "perfect jacket"—the partnering anchor that's right for you.

Minimizing Distractions

Think for a moment about how much noise you listen to every day without recognizing it. Distractions happen constantly and can inhibit listening, building rapport, and staying focused. Minimizing distractions is an important part of getting ready for client interactions.

A workshop participant relates this story: "I had been working with a middle manager for about three months. I found that every time we had a conversation in her office, we never got anywhere. She kept taking phone calls, which interrupted our train of thought. I decided to ask the manager to meet outside of the office for lunch to discuss a project situation. It was so simple and the lunch went great . . . until her cellular phone rang. It was her secretary! After she hung up I jokingly said, "I need to take you hiking in the Grand Canyon to get fifteen minutes of your uninterrupted time!" We laughed as I explained how frustrated I had been over the past three months. The relationship took on a whole new direction. Now we meet outside of her office, and she turns her phone off."

In reviewing the types of distractions you experience, consider the sources of distractions within yourself and from the client and the situation. What inhibits your ability to focus? Table 4.1 lists possible sources of distraction in each category and suggests actions that you can take to minimize them.

Table 4.1. Distractions.

Distractions: Self	Actions you can take to minimize the distraction
• Emotional reaction (such as anger, disappointment, frustration) • Self-doubt • Fear of disappointing the other person or of looking bad • Performance pressure • Personal, family, or health worries	• Share with the other person how you are feeling • Suggest moving the discussion to another time • Ask the other person for coaching or support • Take the time to clear up and process your feelings before the interaction
Distractions: Client	**Actions you can take to minimize the distractions**
• Behaviors you observe in body language or tone of voice (looking at watch, taking phone calls, facial expression, angry or aggressive reactions) • Differing assumptions • Misinformation • Making demands that you cannot fulfill	• Question to clarify what you are observing in the other person's behavior or words • Take the time to discuss assumptions and demands
Distractions: Situation	**Actions you can take to minimize the distractions**
• Time pressure • Interruptions (beeper, phone, people walking by) • Noise • Lack of privacy • Person is talking on cell phone, driving and talking to you all at the same time • Make the time to meet face-to-face	• Clarify time frame and realistic expectations • Ask to speak at a later time • Name the distraction and provide contingency plan • Make a joke about the situation • Communicating by e-mail

	Considerations	*Outcomes*
Define goal going into this interaction	**Focus on:** • What is our outcome for this given the time available? • How would I build trust and commitment?	**Set the stage by:** • Clarifying expectations • Determining allotted time • Agreeing on goal for this interaction • Discussing assumptions

DEFINE YOUR GOALS FOR THE INTERACTION

The second stage of managing client interactions is to define your goal for the interaction. The goal is the focal point that helps you direct the discussion, but it is key to think of the goal as flexible and not as a necessary result—a "nice to have" not a "must have."

A goal can be determined in both spontaneous and preplanned situations. In determining your goal, consider

- The optimum result you want to achieve in this interaction, and
- The way you can use this opportunity to build trust and commitment.

Having at least one goal is critical to influencing the direction of the discussion. Some goals and assumptions should be stated or clarified at the beginning of the interaction, such as how much time is allotted for the discussion. You may have other goals that you should not or do not want to state explicitly, such as making a sale or building rapport.

> *"The greatest thing in this world is not so much where we are, but in what direction we are moving."*
>
> —Oliver Wendell Holmes

John Lingvall, a performance consultant at Bank of America, illustrates the value of goal setting: "With all the changes that are going on with our clients, one of my first goals is to find out what they are going through and how it is working out for them and their team. I find that when I focus on this goal, the senior managers immediately open up and share their true thoughts."

When clarifying your assumptions, stated goals, and unstated goals, think through the following questions:

Operating Assumptions

- What assumptions are you making (about time, equipment, authority, direction)?
- What are you basing your assumptions and conclusions on?
- What assumptions and conclusions do you want to share with the client?
- What assumptions is your client operating under?

Unstated Goals

- How can you further develop trust and a sense of partnering in this interaction?
- Are there areas of resistance you want to understand better?
- How open or closed are you in your own opinions about the situation?

Stated Goals

- Which of your goals for the interaction are you willing to share with the client?
- Based on the time allotted, what can you expect as an optimum result?
- What is the client's goal for the interaction?
- What insights and concerns are you willing to share if the opportunity seems right?

Creating a Common Goal

If you and a teammate are planning a joint discussion with a client, make sure both of you share a common goal for the interaction. This way you will present a united front and help each other and the client stay on track.

 A workshop participant related the following story illustrating the importance of determining a common goal before an interaction: "A colleague and I went on a call together, but we never got around to discussing our goal beforehand. After the meeting, my colleague said that it had been a horrible conversation and that we would never get anywhere with the client. I looked at him with amazement, as I had thought that the call went exceptionally well, and I had met my goal. I learned after the fact that my colleague had gone in with the goal of finalizing a particular decision. No wonder he was upset! Upon reflection, we realized how discussing our goals up front would have been valuable for a couple of reasons. If we had set realistic goals, we could have better supported each other during the meeting. We also would have had a better yardstick for measuring the result."

Setting the Stage Up Front

Does the following situation sound familiar? You've scheduled a one-hour meeting and taken time to prepare your notes and an agenda. The discussion begins with pleasantries about the weather. You quickly review your agenda items and ask everyone if they have anything to add. Numerous people suggest additions to the agenda. Looking at your watch you realize that fifteen minutes have passed, and all you've accomplished so far is catching up on the weather and creating an expanded agenda. You're already behind schedule, and there isn't enough time to get through! You feel rushed and worry that your items won't get the attention they need.

During the first sixty seconds of your client interaction, make sure that expectations of outcomes ("What are we here to accomplish today?") are clarified and that they can be met within the time allotted. It's easy to get caught up in creating an agenda and forget to clarify and agree on goals that can be achieved within the available time frame. To ensure that this doesn't happen, take the following steps:

In the first sixty seconds of any conversation, make sure everyone is ready to converse.

- Clarify expectations for the interaction.
- Determine the allotted time.
- Agree on goals for the interaction based on the time available.
- Discuss assumptions that you and the client have.

Remember that each interaction is a small step forward. Having a common, realistic goal and clearly established parameters and expectations puts you one step closer to optimal results. Just as important, it contributes to building trust and commitment.

Having a clear goal or outcome allows you to be flexible with the agenda and discussion.

CHAPTER HIGHLIGHTS

- Managing client interactions is partnering with others in the moment.

- Interactions provide an opportunity to employ all the consultative roles: partner, strategist, problem solver, facilitator, coach, influencer, technical expert, and administrator and to show your value.

- During interactions, focus simultaneously on three important areas: (1) your own thoughts and reactions; (2) the client's body language, tone of voice, and words; and (3) the general situation (the purpose of your discussion, potential outcomes, and environmental factors).

- Get ready mentally and physically for the interaction by using a partnering anchor and minimizing self, client, and situation distractions.

- Define a goal to guide you in the conversation, remembering that your overall goals are to achieve optimum results and build trust and commitment.

CHAPTER FIVE

FINDING THE SUBJECT

Earlier, you were introduced to the six steps of the Managing Client Interactions Model. In the previous chapter, you learned how to prepare your canvas—how to get ready and define your goal for a client interaction. In this chapter, we'll show you how to manage client interactions by uncovering the many layers of needs, concerns, and perspectives of your clients. You'll begin to apply the art of partnering—reflecting in the moment, staying flexible and focused, and reaching the core issues—to create the most successful client relationships you've ever imagined.

This part of the process is similar to what an artist does when beginning a painting. Before putting brush to canvas or even beginning to mix colors, the painter must discover the true subject of the painting—what is important about what she sees before her. Looking carefully at a landscape, still life, or model—seeing in line and color, the way light falls and forms shadows, the most telling details—reveals the subject to the painter.

This kind of "three-dimensional seeing" is analogous to what you learned to do in Chapter Two: observe your clients' personality, language, opinion/frame of reference, and task approach; be aware of your own reactions; and monitor the level of trust and rapport. Seeing this way enables you to "find the subject" of an interaction—to uncover your client's objectives, concerns, and perspective in a way that adds value to your partnering relationship and moves you closer toward the results you both want to achieve.

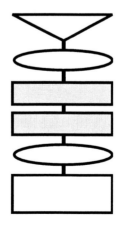

QUESTION

Imagine taking an onion and cutting it in half. What do you see? The multitude of sections inside an onion provide a visual image of the most important part of managing client interactions. "Peeling the onion" is about stripping away layers until you reach core issues and concerns. It's a reminder that every project or initiative is made up of many dimensions, that each layer is an integral

Question	Considerations	Outcomes

Question
To understand opinion/frame of reference and situation
	Ask to determine client's opinion/frame of reference
	• What is important to you about that?
	• What concerns you about that?
	
	Ask to determine desired outcomes for the situation
	• What are key issues now and in future?
	• What would success look like?
		• Peel the onion
		• Question to understand
		  —Client's opinion/ frame of reference
		  —Issues underlying the solution

part of the whole, and that you must work through every layer if you expect to understand truly the opinion and frame of reference of your clients.

You won't know if you don't ask. And if you don't know, you can't add value to your client relationships. Questioning is an essential step of the Managing Client Interactions Model. Keep in mind that the focus during questioning is on understanding the client's objectives, concerns, viewpoint, experiences, and personal insights. In the course of the interaction, continually ask yourself, Do I understand this client's opinion, frame of reference, and the situation so that I can respond appropriately and effectively?

> *"Keep on going and chances are you will stumble on something . . . I have never heard of anyone stumbling on something sitting down."*
>
> —Charles F. Kettering

As an expert in your field, you may have a natural desire to jump in and solve the problem with your expertise, know how, and wonderful ideas. But you may not even know yet what the problem is—what the subject of your painting is. By questioning first, you ensure that your ideas and solutions address the client's needs, concerns, and interests.

Questioning is your opportunity to use a consultative approach to uncover and understand the client's opinion and frame of reference. This requires peeling away layers of issues and concerns to get at what is most important to the client. You need to ask questions about the client's situation and what alternatives and outcomes he or she is considering.

 Jean Roux, a global strategies and health consultant at Levi Strauss and Co., proffers the following advice about questioning: "One thing I have learned is that when I take the time to plan the right questions and the best way of asking them, my chances of being able to influence the client are quite high."

The depth of questioning you are able to pursue will depend upon the time available and the nature of your relationship with the client. In all cases, however, the important thing is to take it one layer at a time. With each layer you peel away, you gain more insight about the situation and client and get closer to the core. Each layer contains a kernel of information that you can use in continuing to ask questions about the topic. Eventually, given enough time, you will reach the core.

Peel the Onion by Asking the Right Questions

To peel the onion to reveal the client's opinion and frame of reference, it helps to observe a few basic principles:

- Ask what, not why.
- Talk outcomes, not problems.
- Focus on the situation by asking what has been tried and what did or did not work.
- Ask the client to be specific.
- Focus on the client by asking value-based questions.

Bill Woodson of Arthur Andersen's Center for Family Business articulates the value of questioning: "I have learned that being consultative means to constantly probe and not take anything at face value. Nine out of ten times the right answer pops up as a result of asking the right questions."

Ask What, Not Why. Questions that ask why tend to put people on the defensive and seem to demand an explanation. They can cause frustration, anxiety, or even anger in the person who is being asked the question. "What" questions, in contrast, encourage introspection and more free-flowing thoughts. They also send a more compassionate message, especially when the questioner's body language and tone of voice are open and interested.

To test this principle, ask people the following questions (or imagine being asked them yourself), and notice the differences in reaction:

- "Why do you feel that way?" versus "What led to your feelings about that?"
- "Why did you make that decision?" versus "What were the factors in your decision?"

Talk Outcomes, Not Problems. In our work with clients, we have noticed that people have a tendency to focus on solving problems rather than on defining desired outcomes. The difference may seem small, but the distinction is powerful. Consider the differences between the questions in each of the following pairs. The first question is outcome-oriented; the second is problem-oriented:

- "What are you trying to accomplish?" versus "Can you describe the problem?"
- "What result do you want to achieve by increasing morale?" versus "What is causing the low morale?"
- "What is it you want your customers to notice or not notice about your service?" versus "What complaints are you hearing that you want to address?"
- "What would you like to accomplish in the meeting?" versus "Which topics should we cover in the agenda?"

Clients are far more interested in reaching desired outcomes than in just solving a problem. If you ask outcome-oriented questions, clients will become more excited, rejuvenated, and focused on possibilities. Problem-oriented questions are useful—even necessary at times—but they often only amplify what is wrong, and they can make people feel detached, hopeless, or overwhelmed. Uncovering clients' desired outcomes enables you to diagnose what is blocking the optimum results and to gain insights about what the client wants to achieve.

Focus on the Situation by Asking What Has Been Tried and What Did or Did Not Work. Questions aimed at uncovering the history of the situation can help you gain a better understanding of the organization, avoid suggestions that were already tried and have failed, and help you generate new ideas. Following are some suggestions of such historical questions:

- "What has been tried?"
- "What is stopping you from . . . ?"

- "What would happen if . . . ?"
- "What are the known and suspected but undetermined problems?"
- "What are your desired outcomes?"

Ask the Client to Be Specific. Sometimes you will need to help people get beyond generalities and focus on deeper levels of information and insight. As you guide the conversation, encourage the client to be more explicit about a topic by using the word *specifically* in the question. For example, "*Specifically,* what bothers you about . . ." or "*Specifically,* what is most important to you in . . ." If the client's response is not precise enough, continue to use the word *specifically* until you are satisfied with the level of detail.

Suzanne's father, Jerry Saxe, has made our point poetically:

> *The English language is quite confusing,*
> *many words mean various things*
>
> *But when it comes to the word specifically,*
> *there is only one bell that rings.*
>
> *When you use the word specifically,*
> *it is definite, explicit, precise*
>
> *There's no room for misunderstanding,*
> *you don't have to explain it twice.*
>
> *Specifically is a particular word,*
> *not like all the rest*
>
> *When you talk specifically,*
> *it's communication at its best.*

Focus on the Client by Asking Value-Based Questions. *Value-based questions* help you peel the onion to get to what is really important to the client. Often clients need help prioritizing and focusing on their main issues and concerns. Value-based questions might include some of the following:

- "What is important to you about . . . ?"
- "What concerns you about . . . ?"
- "If you had to name one [priority, outcome, objective, concern], what would that be?"

Value-based questions help the client close in on a point or issue and are especially helpful with those clients who ramble or who are overwhelmed by their situation or task.

Question to better understand the client and the situation.

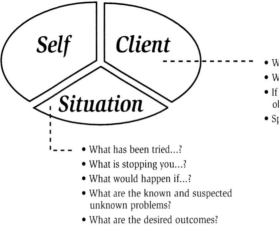

● What is important to you about...?
● What concerns you about...?
● If you had to name (priority, outcome, objective, concern), what would that be?
● Specifically, what do you...?

● What has been tried...?
● What is stopping you...?
● What would happen if...?
● What are the known and suspected unknown problems?
● What are the desired outcomes?

Peeling the Onion—An Example

The following dialogue captures the essence of what a peeling-the-onion conversation might sound like. In this situation, Paula, an internal consultant, is in the middle of the conversation with her primary client, Jim, about the priorities and politics for their project budget. Paula maintains a collaborative tone of voice and positive body language throughout.

> PAULA: Jim, help me to understand which is the higher priority for this project: staying within the budget or meeting the deadline?
>
> JIM: Costs, definitely doing it within the budget.
>
> PAULA: Specifically, what about the costs are you concerned about?
>
> JIM: I'm concerned that the budget will skyrocket if we don't keep close tabs on it.
>
> PAULA: Is there anything else about the budget that is worrying you?
>
> JIM: Well, my manager told me that because of our financial situation last quarter, if we aren't able to come in on budget, the management committee will postpone the second phase of the project until next year.
>
> PAULA: So which is of greater concern: keeping costs down or that the project might be postponed?

JIM: It is actually both, because if we are over budget, the project will surely be postponed. And if the project isn't completed this year, we'll never get more budget for it next year.

PAULA: I see. Are there specific objectives within this project that are most important to you and to the management committee?

JIM: Well, as a matter of fact there are. It is an organizational priority for the new system to both solve our billing problems and provide better customer service by improving the invoicing process.

PAULA: So the most critical components of the project are implementing the new billing process using the new system and making sure customers' needs are met as well?

JIM: Yes, if we could solve the billing fiasco and get feedback from customers that they are happy, senior management would be pleased.

PAULA: If we used your entire budget on just one priority, what would it be?

JIM: Having the customers love what we provide for them. I'm concerned that we have been off target for too long, and now with a slowdown in spending, we may never get there. In thinking about this now, I think if we stayed within budget and did a great job on the billing process, this would give us a chance to demonstrate what we can do, which is about all I could hope for now.

PAULA: How could we show the management committee that this is definitely a spending priority because an investment in this project will improve both invoicing and customer service?

JIM: We need to convince them that making this investment now rather than later is critical to our customers.

And so on. The layers of the onion continue to be revealed! Now that you've read through this dialogue, notice these key elements:

- Paula stayed with the same line of questioning until Jim revealed all that was of concern to him about the topic (the budget). Her questions were phrased just a bit differently each time in order to cast a slightly different light on the topic.

- Paula used value-based questions to get to those that were the core issues from Jim's perspective: (1) funding will run out if the project budget is not managed well; (2) issues beyond his control are affecting the management committee's priorities; (3) improving customer service was very important—in fact, probably the most important issue to Jim.

- Paula used the focusing word *specifically* to take Jim to a deeper level of detail and help him define the most important parts of the project or problem.

- Peeling the onion helped Jim to think more critically about the core issues and to see a potential opportunity for influencing the management committee.

Peel the Onion

For this exercise, you'll need a partner to practice with—a friend, colleague, or family member. Take five minutes and have a conversation in which you ask questions to peel the onion. Select a topic that the person has been struggling with—perhaps a challenge at work or home or a big decision to be made. Set the stage and let your partner know that you want to experiment with having an in-depth conversation. Take notes if you wish.

Remember to do the following:

- Ask what, not why.
- Focus on outcomes rather than problems or issues.
- Ask historical questions to understand the situation fully.
- Encourage the person to be more specific.
- Ask value-based questions to understand fully the person's frame of reference.

When you are finished, reflect on the conversation and make notes on the information and insights you gathered about the person's opinion and frame of reference. Consider which questions led you to a better understanding, and think through future opportunities with this person or with others in which you could use similar questions.

LISTEN

Have you ever noticed that when people describe the attributes of a successful professional, listening effectively is always on the list? The ability to listen well makes people successful, and it can make all the difference in the world in your own client interactions.

Listening gives you the opportunity to further your learning about the person, the situation, and your reaction to both. As you listen, you observe the other person and pay attention to his or her body language, tone of voice, and the words he or she uses. You may not be conscious of it at the time, but

Listen *Determine* *appropriate response* **Look for nonverbal cues**	**Considerations**	**Outcomes**
	Consider: • What else do I need to know to be able to respond to the comments? • What am I missing? • Have I developed rapport?	• Develop rapport through body language, tone of voice, words • Use a partnering filter

this is critical information, and it lends you the insights you need to facilitate the interaction in the moment, develop rapport, and further the relationship.

Understanding Filters

In Chapter Four, we talked about sources of distraction and ways you can avoid them and stay focused. Among the internal sources of distraction that people commonly encounter are filters: preconceived notions, stereotypes, judgments, and expectations that influence what you hear and how you understand it—what twist you put on it.

There is a tendency while listening to others to screen out, consciously or unconsciously, some or all of what is being said. The filters at work at these times are determined by your own opinions and experience—either with this particular person or with other, unrelated people, in similar or dissimilar situations. One primary source of filters is childhood experiences and family background, which influence our frame of reference throughout our adult lives.

> *"You ain't learnin' nothin' when you're doin' all the talkin'."*
>
> —Sign over Lyndon B. Johnson's desk when he was a junior senator

One common filter that most people share is to filter out the positive and focus on the negative. We use the following example in our workshops:

$$2 + 2 = 4 \qquad \text{Lisen} \qquad 8 \div 4 = 3$$

What do you notice about those three things? Most people say that *Lisen* is spelled incorrectly and that 8 divided by 4 equals 2, not 3. And they're right. But no one ever says that 2 plus 2 does equal 4—yet that is equally true.

_____

Here's a real-life example: A meeting we attended recently began with the project manager saying, "We've met three milestones but we missed one." Immediately, all the discussion centered on the milestone that had not been achieved. The successes were discussed only at the last minute, as an afterthought.

_____

Listening filters have many sources, among them

- Stereotypes about race, religion, sex, ethnic background, accent or speech pattern, dress, or mannerisms
- Preconceptions about occupations, such as lawyers or artists, or job level, such as clerk or executive
- Defensiveness due to having been previously criticized or judged
- Expectations or beliefs about how people "ought to" think or act
- Associations made between a person or situation and a person or event in the past
- Assumptions drawn on inadequate information (jumping to conclusions)

Your personal listening filters can cause you to miss important information. Coauthor Virginia LaGrossa tells the following customer service story about filters, which was relayed to her by a branch manager of a bank:

> One very busy Saturday morning, the tellers were doing their best to serve customers and keep the line moving. Suddenly, a man wearing filthy overalls, with dirt on his face and under his fingernails, and an old torn hat falling over his eyes, stepped up to one of the windows. Obviously in a hurry, he said to the teller, "I'd like you to validate my parking ticket." The teller took one very judgmental look at him and abruptly said, "I'm sorry, but we only validate for those doing bank business."
>
> The man replied, "Well, I *am* a bank customer, and I just parked in your lot for five minutes to load my car with compost from the garden store next door." Not believing that he was a customer, the teller repeated that the lot was for those doing bank business, and she would not validate his ticket. In a huff, he left the branch.
>
> The following Monday, the president of the bank received a call from the man, who explained what had happened at the branch. He then told the president he was taking his multimillion-dollar account to another bank—one whose people and policies weren't quite so rigid.

The point of this story is not that the teller should have listened to the multimillion dollar *important* client, but that she made a judgment based solely on his appearance. Furthermore, she used the bank policy as an excuse for not servicing his request. How often do you jump to conclusions about that client who you think is smarter than you, dumber than you, or has more authority than you? Above all, you don't allow your personal filters to get in the way of listening nonjudgmentally. In this story, the bank teller's filters kept her from listening to this customer's needs, asking him questions, and determining an appropriate response. In that one small in-the-moment interaction, she made herself and her whole organization look shabby.

Identifying Your Filters

While it is probably impossible to remove your filters altogether, you can become aware of them so that they interfere as little as possible in your partnering relationships and your goal of achieving optimum results.

Take a moment now and jot down a list of your pet peeves—things that generally bug you when you encounter them in people. Here are some examples:

- People talking very quickly or very slowly
- Someone sitting next to you in the movie theater crunching popcorn loudly.
- Someone ordering food in a restaurant and making substitutions or requesting items "on the side."
- People who wave their hands around when they talk.
- Being put on hold on the telephone.

Most of us can usually go on for quite a while with such a list. Let yourself go.

Now think back to your most recent conversation with your least favorite client. What do you find most difficult or challenging about this client? What pet peeves or prior experiences with this client might have come into play in that exchange? Which filters may have been at work? Be honest and try to sort out your knee-jerk reactions from those that seem like appropriate responses to things the client did or said. Make notes about each category.

Finally, try to imagine how the conversation might have gone had you been able to set aside your filters and listen objectively to the client. Are there questions you could have asked to uncover the client's concerns, or responses you could have made (had you been less defensive, irritated, or dismissive) that would have moved the relationship or the situation forward?

"One of the best ways to persuade others is with your ears—by listening to them."

—Dean Rusk

Lifting Your Filters

The point of the preceding exercise is to be conscious of your filters and to find more productive ways of communicating in the future. It is extremely worthwhile to try to remove the negative filters that might be limiting you and to be objective and open as you focus on understanding the client's opinion and frame of reference.

Lifting your filters is like raising the blinds in a dark room. You let in the light to see better, to get more clarity, and it enables you to stay focused, objective, and interested. The light lets you gather the information you need, which in turn lets you think critically, rather than respond with a knee-jerk or emotional reaction.

To test your efforts at lifting your filters, ask yourself the following questions:

- Have I clearly heard the message and its meaning?
- Did I conscientiously evaluate the message?
- Am I able to respond without judgment or blame?

"Listening" to Body Language, Tone of Voice, and Words

Listening doesn't happen with just your ears; it involves all your senses. Effective listening is really effective observing—"listening with your eyes"—for information about and insights into about what the client is saying. As discussed in Chapter Two, as you listen and observe the overall communication through body language, tone of voice, and words, you are also synthesizing the other person's PLOT: personality, language, opinion/frame of reference, and task approach. Table 5.1 will help you review the different elements to observe in body language, tone of voice, and words.

Listening for Specifics

During an interaction, in addition to observing your client, it can be useful to listen for specific types of information, as the following sections suggest.

Listen to Learn About the Situation. Listen to learn about the makeup of the business, the environment, and the culture of the company. Listen to specific words and phrases the client uses and pay attention to common themes. Then try these words and phrases out on others within the company and gauge their reactions to see whether you are on target.

 As principals of a consulting and training company, we find that one of the most rewarding compliments we hear is "You must work here, you sound just like us." In a recent workshop, a participant commented on our knowledge of the company and industry he worked in. He assumed

Table 5.1. What to Observe in Body Language, Tone of Voice, and Words

	What to Listen for and Observe	**Examples**
Body Language (55 percent of communication)	Facial expressions	Frown, smile, smirk
	Posture	Sloppy, rigid
	Gestures	Expressive, closed
	Breathing, skin, eyes	Fast breathing, blushing, or sweating; rapid blinking; squinting or semi-closed eyes
Tone of Voice (38 percent of communication)	Volume	Loud, soft
	Speed	Fast, slow
	Pitch	High, deep, shrill
	Tone	Angry, frustrated, aggressive, apologetic
Words (7 percent of communication)	Key words	Words the client repeats
	Visual Words (sensing through the eyes)	"I see what you mean" Describes things in pictures
	Auditory Words (sensing through the ears)	"That rings a bell" Describes things in terms of sounds
	Kinesthetic Words (sensing through the body)	"I'm up against the wall" "From your standpoint" Describes things physically

that we had many years of experience in his business, but in fact we were working in his field for the first time. When we told him that, he said, "How do you do it? You really know our company!"

Our answer was pretty simple: We did our homework on the company and its environment. We listened for and learned the language, acronyms, people's names, and expressions. We wove this information into our conversations and presentations so that we could relate to the participants in a very comfortable and familiar manner. The results were instant rapport and respect.

Observing the culture of the company—the habits, norms, and language used—and the environment and work style will give you valuable information. You may do this naturally when traveling in another country. You probably take note of things you might have ignored at home, such as signs, food served in restaurants, or the pace of people walking in the street. Carefully listening for and observing specific words, phrases, issues, and themes allows you quickly to become part of this foreign environment. These observations may be practiced or instinctive, but they're worth their weight in gold, whether you're traveling to another country or simply navigating through a new client company.

When in Rome, do as the Romans do.

It is important to be observant with all your clients, no matter how much you think you know and understand their situation. Next time you visit a client, look around as if you were visiting a foreign country and note things you might ordinarily ignore.

Listen to Calibrate. Another technique for effectively listening and observing is to take stock of your clients' usual physical and emotional reactions, and their unusual ones. If you work with a client regularly, you probably have a sense of how they normally respond in certain situations: when they are happy, frustrated, angry, agreeable, or feeling creative. For example, say you have a client who you know, from past experience, gets very loud when he's angry. The next time he gets loud, you can probably safely assume he might be angry.

Greg Baker, an account manager at Science Applications International Corporation, relates the following story about calibration: "When I first heard of calibration, I wasn't sure if it would be useful. But one day, I realized its value. I was working with a client and noticed that he always got quite agitated when his needs weren't being met.

"About a week later, we were in a meeting, and I could tell that he was getting agitated, so I decided to intervene. I said, 'It seems that we aren't helping you in a way that you need. Can you help us out so that we can in turn help you?' The client stopped dead in his tracks and rapidly calmed down. Then he said, 'Now, that's what I like to hear!'"

Calibrating people's reactions is very much like testing a piece of machinery to determine its baseline and then measuring subsequent reactions against that baseline. The clues for calibrating someone's emotional reactions are shown by the tenor of their body language, tone of voice, and words.

Calibrating Responses

You'll need a partner for the first part of this exercise. Ask a colleague, friend, or family member to do it with you.

Start by asking the person a question that will evoke an emotional response. It can be as simple as "What are some of your favorite foods?" Notice his or her response in terms of body language, tone of voice, and word choice. Then ask "What are some foods you can't stand?" Again watch for the response. Do you notice a difference? You now have baselines for that person's likes and dislikes.

Calibrate your key clients by observing them in the following situations:

- Liking something and then disliking something

- Agreeing with another's opinion and disagreeing with an opinion

- Saying yes and saying no

- Being confused about a situation and understanding a situation

- Feeling overwhelmed and feeling relaxed

Listen for Incongruencies. When you are listening and paying attention to your observations, learn to trust your intuition or "gut reactions." This is often a message to yourself that something isn't quite right—that there's a mismatch or incongruence between what is said and what is conveyed otherwise, most times through body language or tone of voice. You may have missed the cue in your conscious mind.

A vital part of effective listening is to check for incongruencies in the way the client communicates and how you are interpreting what you've observed, heard, and felt. This requires that you periodically reflect in the moment on your own feelings and thoughts and decide on the appropriate response.

What you're really doing here is detective work. Think back to the popular television detective, Columbo. Whenever Columbo sensed an incongruence, he would present his insight in a nonthreatening way. He enlisted the suspect's help to explain what his intuition was telling him by saying, "I'm confused here—could you explain something to me?" Columbo's ability to listen for incongruencies, trust his intuition, and dig to find the root cause are what made him and the television show successful.

Use the following questions to reflect on the incongruencies you observe:

- Is there a contradiction between what the client is saying verbally and his or her body language or tone of voice?

- Is the reaction out of proportion to the importance of the situation?

- Am I feeling mixed emotions or confusion, or sensing something is just not right?

CHAPTER HIGHLIGHTS

- Question to understand the person's opinion and frame of reference:
  - —Ask *what* rather than *why* questions to encourage introspection and more free-flowing thoughts.
  - —Focus your questions on outcomes rather than problems.
  - —Ask what has been tried and what did and did not work to uncover the background of the situation.
  - —Use the word *specifically* to help the client get beyond generalities and focus on deeper levels of information and insight.
  - —Use value-based questions to get to core issues, priorities, and points of view.
- Listening gives you the opportunity to further your learning about the person, the situation, and your reaction to both. As you listen, observe the other person and pay attention to his or her body language, tone of voice, and choice of words.
- Filters reflect your own opinion and frame of reference about the situation and the people involved and are shaped by your previous experiences in similar situations. Listening filters have many sources:
  - —Stereotypes about race, religion, sex, ethnic background, accent or speech pattern, dress, or mannerisms
  - —Preconceptions about occupations or job level
  - —Defensiveness
  - —Expectations or beliefs
- Lifting your filters enables you to ground yourself so that you can stay focused, objective, and open. Ask yourself the following questions:
  - —Have I clearly heard the message and its meaning?
  - —Did I conscientiously evaluate the message?
  - —Am I able to respond without judgment or blame?
- "Listen" to body language, tone of voice, and words to synthesize the other person's message, feelings, and distractions.
- Calibrate your clients' reactions to determine a baseline for certain situation and gauge the strength of subsequent reactions.
- Listen for incongruencies and trust your intuition by periodically reflecting in the moment on your own feelings and thoughts.

CHAPTER SIX

PAINTING WHAT YOU SEE

In the preceding two chapters you were introduced to the six steps of the Managing Client Interaction Model. You learned how to get ready and define your goal for the current interaction. Then you learned how to ask questions, to "peel the onion," to get to the core of issues, information, and attitudes. Finally, you learned how to listen to your client's response objectively and in the context of that client's usual style of interaction.

Two further communication skills complete the interaction model: refining your goal and responding. These skills can have a dramatic impact on your ability to interact successfully with your client. They are, in effect, where the art of managing a client interaction yields a tangible result, where the exchange most clearly moves forward—where you begin to "paint what you see" so that the client can see it as well.

REFINE YOUR GOAL FOR COMPLETING THE INTERACTION

The next critical stage in your client interaction is to assess an appropriate goal for completing the interaction. Fortunately, you already have most of the information you need to make this determination based on having peeled the onion to understand the client's opinion and frame of reference and the situation. Also, during your interactions you have listened and made observations you can factor in when deciding on your next step.

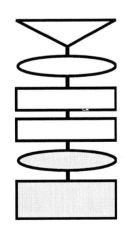

In making an in-the-moment determination about the most appropriate goal, during the interaction, periodically reflect on the following questions:

- Do I need to adjust my initial goal? If so, how? Should it be smaller, broader, more inclusive, more exclusive? Should it focus on the situation, the person, or how we are working together?

Refine goal for completing this interaction

Considerations

Consider:

- Where do I go from here?

Outcomes

- Determine if you can achieve initial goal
- Establish next strategic move

"To be successful is to achieve an objective, but to be a success is always to have yet another objective in mind."

—Anonymous

- What is the best response I can give or question I can ask at this point?
- What is my next strategic move in terms of the time available and what I have learned so far?

RESPOND

Now that you have prepared your canvas and posed your subject—learned from questioning and observing your client—the ultimate in-the-moment opportunity in the interaction has arrived: it's time for you to respond to your client, to begin painting. Will this be your moment of brilliance? At this point you have learned a great deal about the client, the situation, and how you think of and feel about the situation. This is your opportunity to show your artistry and demonstrate that you have not only been paying attention but that you have good ideas, solid suggestions, and more thought-provoking questions.

Respond
Apply expertise
Confirm understanding
Broaden client's opinion/ frame of reference
Recommend next steps

Considerations

- Use partnering language
- Continue to build rapport
- Share your experience and observations
- Offer suggestions
- Check out what is realistic
- Use metaphors, stories, analogies

Outcomes

Respond by focusing on all aspects

- Client's frame of reference
- Your feelings and perceptions
- The situation

When responding focus on..

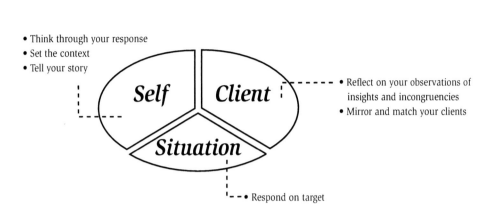

• Think through your response
• Set the context
• Tell your story

Self | **Client**

Situation

• Reflect on your observations of insights and incongruencies
• Mirror and match your clients

• Respond on target

Figure 6.1. Responding Based on Self, Client, and Situation.

Figure 6.1 shows possible ways to respond, taking into account the three areas of client, situation, and self. Responding is an art in itself. It requires a combination of tact, flexibility, caution, assertiveness, intuition, partnership, and knowledge. The techniques we suggest on the following pages are designed to help you become skilled in this art.

Thinking Through Your Response

Thinking about *what* to say is one thing you need to consider; the other is *how* to say it. While mentally preparing your response, make sure you are not actually censoring yourself—either by minimizing the value of what you have to say or by being defensive or reactive, which can prevent you from fully telling your story.

When you are self-censoring, you think things like, "I'd better not say that," or "I am right, and she is wrong." In thinking like this, rather than being consciously reflective, you sabotage yourself. Here are a few more examples of thoughts that might be familiar if you sometimes censor yourself:

- It is important to be right, no matter if it hurts others' feelings.
- It is important not to hurt others' feelings.
- I'll just ignore it, and it will go away.
- I am not to blame.
- He won't listen to me anyway.

- She doesn't respect me or my organization.
- I shouldn't express my feelings or emotion.
- He or she is [more senior, more powerful, wiser, richer] and therefore must know better than I do.
- I don't share information unless I get something in return.

The challenge is to overcome these inner thoughts so that you can stay in the moment and focus on the information and insights you have gleaned from this interaction and other experiences. It is trusting your own reactions, perspective, and insights that allows you to make a difference to your client. By responding from your heart and gut this way, you make it safer for the client to express himself or herself more honestly.

Andrea Dee, a project controller at Science Applications International Corporation, expresses this approach: "I have a completely new orientation now. I used to bring only 'my expertise' to work. Now I am relationship-oriented and focus on how we are going to work together and build our trust and commitment in order to achieve the best results. I love that."

Setting the Context

Setting the context for your response is an important part of enabling the client to listen openly to your ideas. Knowing the context or background positions what you say and puts it in perspective. For example, a difficult but common situation is when you want to prepare the client for harsh realities you know are ahead. You might say, "This is a difficult situation we are in, and I have learned a great deal from listening to you. First, I want to thank you for being so frank and honest. I would like to summarize as truthfully as I can the situation as I see it." By the time you have set the context this way, the listener should be ready to hear your honest words and truthful analysis of the situation. If, on the other hand, you had responded without setting the context, the client might not be prepared to listen openly.

Another situation in which setting the context can be helpful for the listener is when the client does not have the same depth of experience you do or is not familiar with your background or the history of your project. In these cases it can be helpful to give a brief update or summary to precede your response.

Telling Your Story

In Chapter Three we emphasized the need to be succinct and relevant in sharing your Expertise Statements. However, sometimes an opportunity arises in which you can make your point most effectively by telling a story through metaphor, personal recollection, analogy, or examples.

Jon Olson, a managing director with Arthur Andersen, uses the following analogy to communicate to tax managers what it takes to be seen as a business advisor: "Right now, we are viewed as a 'compliance tax practice.' Our clients ask us for a box, and they get a box. In fact, it is a great box. But instead, we should be giving our clients a circle, because it is what they need to impact behavior. During the process of developing the circle with our clients, we need to influence them that this is the right way to go. We provide something that they didn't expect. We then move from compliance or order takers to consultants and business advisors."

Make Your Point

Here are a few simple tips for how to use stories, metaphors, and analogies to make your point:

- Use your personal experiences as a basis for storytelling.
- Set the story up by painting a picture of the scene. Use descriptive words and dramatic tone and gestures to get the total effect.
- Make your key points succinct and poignant. Get rid of extraneous descriptions.
- Change the stories in order to make a point. Embellish or exaggerate the story to make it compelling.
- Analogies or well-known quotes can be used as themes. For example, "The journey is the destination."
- Pick metaphors that the listener can relate to. Areas of common interest or knowledge often provide good metaphors. Competing in a sport, playing a musical instrument, raising a family, building a house, or planning for a trip might all be possible metaphors for planning, implementation, and communication issues.

Reflecting on Your Insights
and Observations of Incongruencies

Your own observations and sense of things can provide a quite powerful message. We have found the following to be important and effective in sharing observations and insights:

Sharing Observations

- Make sure the client is open to hearing your thoughts.
- Ask for permission: "I've been sitting here a while listening. I wonder if it would be appropriate to share what I have been observing and noticing."
- Be honest, open with your insights, and thoughtful about not putting people in a corner or on the defensive. Point out incongruent behavior (mixed messages) and peel the onion for additional information. The way to do this is to phrase the observations so that they are about the behavior and not the person: "I'd like to pause for a minute and share something I have been observing as we have been talking. When we discuss Mary's role on the project team, you seem to skirt the issue. Do you have concerns I should know about?"
- Share your own experiences in relation to what you have observed: "This situation reminds me of a similar project in which we ran into the same sort of obstacle. We were unable to get all the key players in the room at once and reach consensus. We spent weeks getting everyone's input separately and lost precious time."
- If your client appears to be in conflict or confused about a particular topic, offer your observations. You might do this in such a way that you assume the responsibility and feeling of confusion: "I am finding as we talk that I am getting more confused about what it is we are trying to accomplish. I am hearing all sorts of different things. Would it be okay with you if we take a few minutes to revisit our objectives and see if they are still relevant?"

Mirroring and Matching

Using mirroring and matching, as described in Chapter Two, can also help make it easier for your listeners to hear you, because you are communicating to them in their natural mode. Your clients will think you understand them and that you are easy to talk with. An additional benefit is that you will understand the client better. Try the following suggestions when responding to clients:

Mirror and Match Your Client

- Listen for key words that the client uses repeatedly. What does the client call employees, staff people, associates, team members, workers? Use those words in your response.

- Observe whether the client uses visual, auditory, or kinesthetic words. Try responding in the same mode. For visual types, paint a picture in words. For auditory people, try phrases such as *sounds like, I hear you, clear as a bell.* For those most comfortable with physical images, try phrases such as *it feels to me, solid as a rock,* or *we can nail it down.* If the client expresses himself or herself in flat, analytical language, mirror that in your response.

- Notice the pace, pattern, or tone in which certain things are stated. Change the volume, speed, or pitch of your voice to match that of your client.

- Make note of the person's posture and any gestures he or she may use. Once you notice these elements, mirror them. If he or she leans forward, you lean forward. If the person crosses his or her legs, cross yours.

Responding on Target

The techniques just described—being reflective, setting the context, telling your story, responding based on your observations of insights and incongruencies, and mirroring and matching—all help to create open communication and a sense of partnering. Now that you are ready to respond, you have a variety of approaches you can take based on your refined goal for the interaction.

- *Apply your expertise.* Use Expertise Statements to hook the client into listening to other approaches and options.
- *Confirm your understanding.* Respond by confirming your understanding of the situation before you move on. This provides you with an opportunity to clarify assumptions and make sure that no one has other hidden agendas or unstated goals.
- *Broaden the client's opinion/frame of reference.* In your responses, look for ways to broaden your client's point of view so that he or she will be more open to the best possible solution. Your insights can enlighten him or her to think beyond traditional approaches or immediate results. By providing options, you offer choices that help the client feel better about making decisions.

"Perseverance is a great ele-ment of success. If you only knock long enough and loud enough at the gate you are sure to wake up somebody."

—Henry Wadsworth Longfellow

• *Recommend next steps.* If you want to propel a client toward making a decision, focus on next steps. These could be next steps for the current interaction (to change the agenda or topic) or follow-up action items for after the interaction.

Keep persevering in your client interactions. If you are encountering resistance, adapt your approach. Use the Managing Client Interaction Model, tools, and techniques to help you optimize your results and build trust and commitment.

CHAPTER HIGHLIGHTS

- In order to make an in-the-moment determination about the most appropriate goal, think about the following questions during the interaction:
  - —Do I need to adjust my initial goal and, if so, how?
  - —What is the best response I can give or question I can ask at this point?
  - —What is my next strategic move in terms of the time available and what I have learned so far?
- Thinking about *what* to say is one part of responding and being mindful of *how* to say it is the other part. While mentally preparing your response make sure you are not actually self-censoring.
- Setting the context for your response is an important part of enabling the client to openly listen to your ideas. Knowing the context or background puts what you say in perspective and positions it.
- Tell your story through metaphors, personal recollections, analogies, and examples.
- Reflect on your observations of insights and incongruencies:
  - —Make sure the client is open to hearing your thoughts.
  - —Be honest, open with your insights, and thoughtful about not cornering people.
  - —Share your own experiences in relation to what you have observed.
  - —If your client appears to be in conflict or confused regarding a topic, offer your observations.

- Mirror and match your client's body language, tone of voice, and words with your own. Behaviors you might mirror and match are use of words, posture, and pacing or speech patterns.
- Respond on target:
  —Apply your expertise.
  —Confirm understanding.
  —Broaden the client's opinion/frame of reference.
  —Recommend next steps.

PART THREE

JOURNEY TO SUCCESS

The Consultative Process

Over the last decades, various models of project management, product development, organizational development, quality improvement, and consulting were much talked about and became widely used in businesses. In consulting, two well-known models were Peter Block's internal consulting model (1981) and Gordon Lippitt and Ronald Lippitt's 1986 six-step consulting process. Marvin Weisbord's Six-Box Model (1978) was used for organizational diagnosis, as was McKinsey and Company's 1982 Seven-S Framework (Peters and Waterman, 1982). In addition, the Total Quality Improvement twelve-step and ten-step processes were introduced as ways of problem solving and improving processes and results. More recently, salespeople have used such models as Robert Miller's and Stephen Heiman's *Strategic Selling* (1987) and Neil Rackham's *Spin Selling* (1988). Similarly, product development and project management professionals also have models and processes they use to align themselves with consulting projects.

Over our years as trainers, consultants, and managers we have used these models in working both with professionals in accounting, engineering, financial services, and sales and with clients who developed and marketed products and services. (Since then we have surveyed our colleagues and clients on the models' application and use.) We began to notice how many of these processes and models required elaborate steps that were perfect for organizational diagnosis but not helpful to individuals or teams. Our clients began to tell us that what they needed was straightforward, practical approaches to help their professionals (both internal and external) be more consultative in working with clients. The process needed to be flexible enough to work in all types of situations, and it needed to collapse and expand like an accordion—the essence of working as partners remaining intact regardless of the scope of the project.

Our challenge was to come up with such a process: one that could be used in the fast-paced world of today's work environment; one that would be applicable to professionals in all fields and was simple, memorable, practical, and user-friendly. To that end, we looked closely at the various approaches listed above as well as those used by successful professionals—engineers, quality improvement experts, instructional technologists, salespeople, and project managers—and found that, although diverse, these people had something in common. They all used a systematic yet flexible methodology for planning and implementing their work, and they factored into their processes strategies for gaining input and commitment from others and opportunities for expanding and applying their expertise.

Out of this research came the four phases of the Consultative Process, which we developed and refined to meet our clients' needs. Over the years, we have simplified and honed the process in response to market needs and the input of thousands of workshop participants in numerous companies, who have found it to work very well. The four chapters in this part of the book describe the phases of the Consultative Process and discuss integration of the various elements key to working more effectively with people and applying your expertise to show your value. The paragraphs that follow introduce the four phases and the activities involved in each phase.

PHASES OF THE CONSULTATIVE PROCESS

In Chapter One we described The Consultative Approach as a balance of people, process, and expertise used to produce optimum results and build trust and commitment. We want to reinforce that maintaining this balance is a conscious and deliberate effort on your part. In using the Consultative Process, you will be balancing what you need to accomplish with how you go about producing an optimum result. This process emphasizes both the strategic and tactical aspects of planning and executing your projects, tasks, and assignments. By design, it can be adapted to most work situations so that you can use it both for relatively straightforward assignments, such as setting up a meeting, and for complex projects such as organizationwide implementation of a new system.

The diagram of the Consultative Process model illustrates its systematic yet dynamic and flexible nature. The four phases are cyclical, representing the iterative nature of work. The word *feedback* is shown at the center because it is the driving force for each phase and provides a reminder to stay connected with your various client groups.

Each phase has several key activities that describe the focus, strategies, and partnering opportunities you need to consider. The chapters in Part Three provide detailed information, tools, techniques, and exercises for each phase and activity. But first, let's look at an overview of each phase.

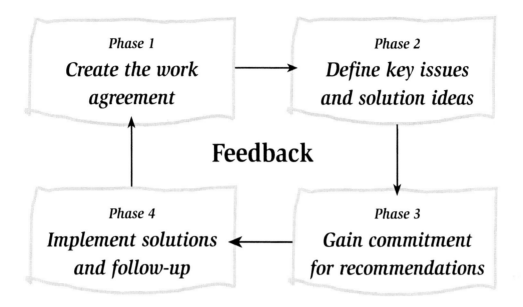

The Consultative Process.

Phase 1: Create the Work Agreement

- Key Activity 1: Understand the client's business and needs.
- Key Activity 2: Conduct a work agreement discussion.
- Key Activity 3: Develop and communicate the work agreement.

Phase 1 of the Consultative Process—Create the Work Agreement—is one that you'd probably recommend based on your own experience. Initiating a project or task with a common understanding and agreement is a great place to start. It begins with you understanding your client's business and discussing your client's issues, needs, and situation. With this knowledge, you are positioned to make a clear, concise work agreement that outlines expectations from all parties regarding what is to be accomplished and how you will work together. The nature of the work dictates how simple or complex the agreement needs to be. Thus, the steps you take to create a work agreement can be straightforward, quick, and compact or more complex or compound, requiring various tasks and more time, people, and thought.

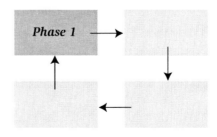

Phase 2: Define Key Issues and Solution Ideas

- Key Activity 1: Determine information and insight areas to explore with all client groups.
- Key Activity 2: Discuss key issues and brainstorm solution ideas with all client groups.
- Key Activity 3: Discuss key issues and solution ideas with the primary client.

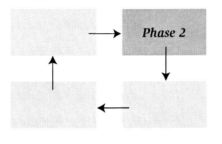

This phase of the Consultative Process is about gathering information and insights from all client groups. The goal is to understand both your clients' needs and concerns and any potential obstacles so that you can develop possible solutions. As a part of this phase, you will plan how to get feedback and input from the various client groups and translate your learning into solutions that can be implemented.

Phase 3: Gain Commitment for Recommendations

- Key Activity 1: Prepare for recommendations discussion.
- Key Activity 2: Discuss information, insights, and recommendations.
- Key Activity 3: Gain agreement on next steps.

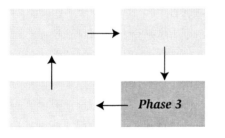

Now the time has come to share the information and insights you gleaned in Phase 2, outline your recommended solutions, and get agreement for implementation. The focus of this phase is on developing a strategy for getting a commitment to your recommendations and moving the project or task to the implementation phase. The key is to understand your clients' business issues and concerns well so that you can relate the benefits and value of your ideas and recommendations.

Phase 4: Implement Solutions and Follow Up

- Key Activity 1: Consider organizational, operational, and individual issues.
- Key Activity 2: Identify readiness, rollout, and reinforcement activities.
- Key Activity 3: Develop the implementation map.

Implementation planning includes the integration of organizational, operational, and individual success factors into a game plan. The magnitude of implementation efforts depends on the complexity of the solutions, anticipated obstacles, and available resources. The Implementation Map you will create will focus on planning a well-conceived rollout that creates readiness for the solution and ensures reinforcement.

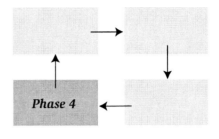

Like most professionals, you probably already use a process and a variety of techniques to ensure success in your work. We offer our methodology as a way to reflect on your client and project situations and identify areas where you want to produce even better results. Our process builds on the models mentioned at the beginning of this section and on the work of many others that have come before, adapting those techniques to the world of the twenty-first century. We hope you enjoy using this process and believe you will be astounded with the results.

CHAPTER SEVEN

GOING IN THE SAME DIRECTION

This chapter leads you through the process of creating a work agreement, Phase 1 of the Consultative Process. We can't emphasize the value of work agreements enough. They're easy to create, and they save you time, money, and all the headaches that can occur when each party has a different expectation or idea about what has been agreed to. The professionals we interviewed consistently mentioned work agreements (written or verbal) as a critical factor to the success of a project. Why? Because work agreements provide a basis for communication, understanding, and commitment where it counts most—at the very beginning. They can head off most of your people and project problems. They ensure that you and your client are headed in the same direction.

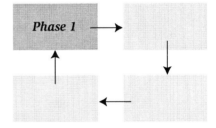

Joyce Bennett, total quality manager at United Defense, tells this story about the value of work agreements: "Once in a great while, I don't have time to develop a formal or even informal work agreement with my clients. Within a few days, however, I find myself asking 'What's the matter? Something isn't right.' The answer always goes back to expectations not being clear.

"When this happened recently, I went back to the client and asked them for a meeting in which we could discuss how we were going to work together and what they expected. It was like a 'rebirth of the project.' Once the meeting was over, we both felt clear and ready to roll and agreed to check in periodically to make sure we were still on track. I know that when I don't create a work agreement up front, I get into trouble!"

Think back to some typical business frustrations you have experienced, and you'll see why work agreements make sense. Do any of the following situations sound familiar?

- You attend a meeting with others and afterward find out that everyone has come away with a different understanding of what was decided.

- You work incredibly hard to prepare a report, proposal, or presentation, and your reward is the response "This isn't what I expected, and it doesn't meet my needs!"

- You form a new team, and a lot of time is wasted before the team members figure out why the group was formed, who is responsible for what, and how all the activities will interconnect.

- You are in the middle of an assignment when your client changes the scope—but still expects you to meet your deadline.

Situations such as these happen all the time. In our workshops we have heard numerous examples that illustrate the point—some humorous, some tragic, and some downright pitiful. All these stories remind us that creating a work agreement up front will go a long way toward minimizing—even preventing—miscommunication, confusion, redundant work, and frustration for you and for your client groups. Work agreements ensure that the project starts off moving toward an optimum result.

WHAT IS A WORK AGREEMENT?

There's no magic required in creating work agreements, just common sense. Typically, the work agreement is made between you and your primary client or team members to clarify what you will be doing, how you will be working together, and the results you collectively expect to produce. The work agreement summarizes objectives, roles, responsibilities, resources, and deliverables. It ensures that there is understanding and commitment among all parties.

Figure 7.1 shows several categories of work agreements appropriate to a range of situations, from formal to informal, simple to complex. A good rule of thumb is that the more straightforward the situation, the less detailed the work agreement. The more complicated the project, the more people you will want to involve and the more precise you will want to be; that is to say, you will want to write a formal contract. A contract is most beneficial when

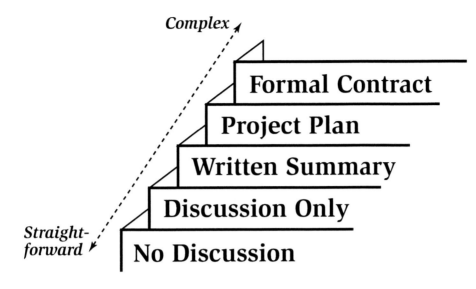

Figure 7.1. Categories of Work Agreements.

created at the beginning of a project and updated throughout. This ensures that you and your clients are working under the same operating assumptions and expectations.

Formal Contract

A *contract* is a formal work agreement usually written to define the delivery of products or services from one entity to another. A contract might cover such areas as specifications, terms and conditions, liabilities, and financial arrangements. An internal contract might be called a service level agreement. An external contract might be called a commitment letter or statement of work. If you work with formal contracts, consider adding a project plan as an addendum, to outline how you and the client will work together.

Project Plan

Typically, a *project plan* describes a detailed project or work assignment that requires the use of a variety of resources. In some organizations, a project plan is required for funding and appropriation of resources. Teams will find a project plan particularly helpful in organizing and executing their work, defining roles and responsibilities, establishing timelines and due dates, and determining resources and deadlines.

Written Summary

Follow-ups to meetings or conversations, quick confirmations, and status reports—by memo or e-mail—fall into this category of work agreement. A *written summary* keeps others aware of information that affects them and ensures that expectations, roles, and responsibilities are understood by all parties.

Discussion Only

We refer to verbal agreements you make during interactions for which there is no subsequent written communication as *discussion-only* work agreements. You probably make hundreds of these kind of agreements in the course of a week in person and on the phone.

To avoid ending such interactions with differing assumptions and understandings, conclude the conversation with a quick verbal summary of what was agreed to, who's doing what, and how long it will take. Also, when you have made a discussion-only agreement, listen to your intuition. You may want to send a follow-up e-mail to confirm the conversation. A written summary, even a quick one, will verify that everyone is on the same track. It's worthwhile insurance—for your project and for your peace of mind.

No Discussion

The most informal type of work agreement is the *no-discussion* agreement. It is typically a voice mail or e-mail communication. While these agreements are convenient, they can also be risky. Pay attention to how much you rely on this medium in your busy schedule. For straightforward tasks, a discussion of specifics may not be necessary. But for more complex information, differing assumptions can become a problem. Also, without discussion you lose the opportunity to ask questions or to make observations of the other person and apply your expertise.

No-discussion is no-hassle, but it leaves a lot to be desired. Remember, your goal is to make sure that everyone is operating under the same set of assumptions. If you don't allow yourself the opportunity for clarification, you may have to backtrack and create consensus down the road, when it can be more difficult.

A client of ours, Katy, shared an experience about the importance of clarifying what might seem like obvious details. Katy is responsible for PC training for several divisions within her company. A manager called her to schedule new software training for his staff. He followed up by e-mail with a list of employees and dates that would be convenient. Since it was so straightforward, Katy set up the class without any further interaction.

During the training, Katy observed that the employees were bored and in some cases resistant and angry. She stopped the class and asked what was wrong. Their responses were alarming: "I don't know why I'm here." "This software has nothing to do with my job." "I already know this program." She was astounded and felt stupid when she found out that the manager had not told his staff why they were attending the training. Worse, they would not even be getting the new software for another two months.

This story illustrates the pain and frustration that can result from not defining assumptions, expectations, roles and responsibilities, and the best process to produce optimum results. Even if you think that your agreement is relatively straightforward, you have no way of knowing what the other person understands unless you discuss and confirm.

THE CONSULTATIVE ROLES OF PHASE 1

In creating work agreements with your primary client and team members, you have an opportunity to demonstrate all the Consultative Roles:

- *Problem solver*—identifying red flags and potential concerns and issues
- *Strategist*—identifying business issues and concerns and how the project or assignment relates to organizational priorities
- *Facilitator*—managing the discussion so that what you need to know to understand and plan the project or task gets discussed
- *Technical expert*—identifying discussion topics and making recommendations on the project process that will produce optimum results
- *Coach*—assisting others during the discussion to make sure they understand their roles, responsibilities, and commitments
- *Influencer*—persuading others to consider different approaches
- *Administrator*—preparing and organizing the agenda for the discussion
- *Partner*—demonstrating flexibility and openness to ideas and input

KEY ACTIVITIES FOR PHASE 1

Creating a work agreement in the initial stage of your project, task, or assignment, consists of three key activities:

- Key Activity 1: Understand the client's business and needs
- Key Activity 2: Conduct a work agreement discussion
- Key Activity 3: Develop and communicate the work agreement

Use these key activities as a guide for clarifying expectations, roles, and responsibilities during Phase 1.

Key Activity 1: Understand the Client's Business and Needs

For clients to view you as a business partner, they must believe that you have a good working knowledge of them and their business. This means that you must do your homework on the strategies, concerns, practices, and priorities that your clients worry about. Think of ways you can gather this information before meeting with the client to discuss the work. The following list provides you with a starting place. Having done this research up front you will ask better questions to understand the client's needs, concerns, and priorities.

Tips for Understanding the Client's Business

- Read the company's annual report, newsletter, and marketing brochures.
- Access the company's web page—often—to obtain company information. If you subscribe to an on-line service you may have additional resources available. For example, America Online provides business databases such as Hoover's Business Reports.
- Read the same publications your client reads. Scan industry journals to read between the lines, watching for advertisements by competitors and announcements of similar products and services. Read respected business journals such as the *Harvard Business Review, Fortune, Forbes,* and *Business Week.* And don't forget the newer, cutting-edge journals such as *Fast Company.* Read business-oriented books of interest to your client.

- Ask people in the industry and company to name the top three business trends affecting the industry and company. This can also open up avenues of conversation you would not have anticipated.

- Learn about the client's world firsthand by getting into the day-to-day operating environment. Take a tour of the client's business operations or headquarters. If the client has retail outlets, shop them. If you are consulting with internal clients and their offices are separate from yours, go visit that facility and have lunch in their cafeteria. You would be amazed at what you can learn.

- Learn the purpose of the client's organization. How do they make money or support the company in making money? How are they evaluated?

- Find out about the prevailing corporate culture, political environment, management style, and internal language or jargon.

By understanding your client's business and organization you not only add value, but you develop much better client rapport. Taking the time to familiarize yourself with your client's business enables you to jump-start your discussion: you won't have to start the conversation with the same tired old "tell-me-about-your-business" question.

Judy Estey, vice president and marketing director of CB Commercial Real Estate, told us the following story: "In preparing a presentation for a major flower mart, a real estate broker recognized that the competition was asking questions of the usual people in the senior management ranks. The broker decided that he needed to do something different to truly understand the business, issues, and needs. For two nights in a row, he and his team put on their sweatshirts, rolled up their sleeves, and worked the loading docks of the flower mart from 10:30 P.M. to 4:30 A.M. They talked to the loading dock people, the transportation people, the delivery folks, and the flower vendors. In doing so they gathered an enormous amount of information about the business, the issues, the employees' opinions, and a variety of solution ideas. Using this information, they stood out from the rest, as they truly understood the business—and they were successful in obtaining the job."

Key Activity 2: Conduct a Work Agreement Discussion

Conducting a work agreement discussion gives you the opportunity to link your knowledge about the business and your expertise to the client's challenges. During the discussion, bridge the gap between abstract ideas and the current situation. Focus on the actual scope of work.

"Good listeners generally make more sales than good talkers."

—B. C. Holwick

To ensure that the time you have with the client is well spent, consider the following tips for preparing for these discussions, whether you are meeting face-to-face or by phone.

Tips for Conducting a Work Agreement Discussion

- Determine who should be involved in the first meeting or discussion. Will all the key players who represent the project, task, or assignment be present? Often the needs and interests of peripheral-yet-important team members—not to mention the all-important end users—get overlooked in this discussion.

- Agree ahead of time on the agenda and how much time is needed. Avoid getting into situations in which the client is too distracted to focus on specifics. The time you plan for the discussion needs to correspond to the complexity of the work.

- Assess the client's understanding of and sense of urgency about the work. A client will often have already identified a solution to a problem and designated you to implement that solution. In that case, the client should have plenty of information and insight to share. But what if the client or team is looking to you for direction and focus? In that case, your timeline may need to factor in a learning curve for your client. You may need to be prepared to educate your client about the nature of the work, his or her role, your needs, and how you would like to work together to achieve the desired results.

- Plan Expertise Statements that you might want to use during this interaction.

- Think of areas to explore with the client (or anyone else present) to peel the onion and develop insights about potential concerns or issues.

- Complete a PLOT on those who will be attending the meeting. Determine your strategy for how to partner effectively.

Kirsten Alston, a performance consultant at Bank of America, describes the tack she and her colleagues take in these business discussions to establish their value: "Many people in human resources do not have a business background, so we come across as not being able to talk the client's language. We were human resources people first, using terms such as *front-end analysis* rather than *understanding the client's needs.* As we move to more of a consulting business, we are talking to our clients more about their business, concerns, and issues. My value comes from knowing human resources *and* knowing my client's business."

Question Background, Current Situation, and Scope of Work

Create a questioning strategy to further your understanding of the client's business and needs and what you need to know in order to commit to the project, task, or assignment. Taking a few minutes to create an agenda will pay off immeasurably in making the most of the time and ensuring that you cover all the bases.

Use what you have learned from experience to customize areas to explore, and don't forget to "peel the onion" to get to the client's opinion and frame of reference. We suggest that your questioning strategy cover three general areas: background, current situation, and scope of work. Background and current situation provide a context and overview of the work. The scope of work should summarize what is agreed to for the project.

The suggested topics that follow provide a starting place for you to develop a questioning strategy for gathering information and insights. Use the ideas presented here, add your own, and ignore those that don't apply to you.

Background areas cover the big-picture aspects of your client's business, including strategic focus, organizational factors, and line of business. Ask background questions every time you meet with the client to keep up-to-date and to expand your awareness. Background topics include the following:

- Business vision, goals, and strategic direction
- Financial situation and measures
- Trends in the marketplace regarding customers, competition, and global issues

- Organization style, culture, and human resource philosophy
- Organizational structure
- Company operations
- Products and services life cycle

Current situation areas include the factors leading to the business rationale for the work you are doing, the people with whom you will be working, and the overall readiness to meet the goals. Investigate the following:

- Connection of this work to background and reasons why the work is a priority at this time
- Client's experience with subject or project and with you
- Client's PLOT (especially opinion/frame of reference for the situation or project)
- Readiness of the client, the organization, and customers to meet the goals
- Means of measuring success
- Implementation and/or integration assumptions

Scope of work topics are the specific points included in the work agreement itself that outline the agreed-on expectations. Depending on the situation, all these topics may not be appropriate for your project or task, but keep them in mind when defining the work with your client to make sure you don't miss anything. They apply in straightforward situations and in detailed project plans. The key is to cover the scope of work to the extent possible and make sure that there is a clear understanding between you, the primary client, and team members.

When writing your work agreements, consider the following topics. Not all of them will apply to every situation, but they provide a starting place for you to create your own template.

Work Agreement Topics

- *Background/current situation:* Describe the project or work, background, and why it is a priority at this time.
- *Objectives:* Summarize what the final results or outcomes of the effort are expected to be.
- *Deliverables:* Describe in detail the final product or service, level of quality, and specifications.

- *Schedule:* Outline key milestones and due dates. Determine whether the schedule or milestones will change as new information is provided.

- *Roles and responsibilities:* List who is responsible for what and by when according to the schedule. This is especially important if you need to justify the resources you've used. For large and complex projects, consider developing a team matrix listing everyone's role for the duration of the project.

- *Process used to meet objectives:* Describe the phases and steps that are appropriate and how the client or team will be involved in the process. This aspect of the work agreement is particularly important, because often the size of the effort may be underestimated by others who are not familiar with or involved in enough detail to appreciate how long things can take. This discussion also allows you the opportunity to indicate the points in the process at which the client or team must be involved in decision making or status updates.

- *Resources required:* List the number of people, type of facilities, administrative support, and special equipment or tools you will need to get the job done.

- *Budget or costs:* Outline internal and external costs and outside purchases. A budget is usually required as part of a project plan's approval. If you are not familiar with the budgeting process, ask your manager or client if there are templates you should use.

- *Status reporting:* Describe the method and frequency with which the client or team will be kept informed of progress, updates, problems, and necessary changes or corrections. This aspect provides the opportunity to involve certain people intermittently over the life of the project or assignment.

- *Success criteria:* List success measures based on indicators such as return on investment and productivity or performance improvement. Consider interim and terminal measures and comparisons against other results. Ask your clients what they think success will look like.

- *Assumptions:* Outline your understanding of the assumptions on which the work agreement is based. This can be one of the most important aspects of the conversation. Include factors that will affect the process and final outcome, such as availability of resources, turn-around time for reviews, data-gathering requirements, schedule, and budget.

Preparing for a Work Agreement Discussion

Select a client with whom you want to write a work agreement. Using the background, current situation, and scope of work categories, prepare specific questions that you want to ask. If you are unfamiliar with some areas of the client's business, plan to explore them further. You may need clarification on some topics, such as your understanding of your role or the budget. Plan a balance of strategic and tactical questions, since the tendency is to focus on the latter. Remember, this is your opportunity to be viewed as a strategist and a business partner—not just as a technical expert and administrator—so consider Expertise Statements you might make as well.

After you meet with the client, make note of what you learned and which questions generated the most information and insights. Add those questions to your personal library of questions. Refine your Expertise Statements so that you are able to say them succinctly and spontaneously.

Key Activity 3: Develop and Communicate the Work Agreement

Following the discussion in which you define the scope of work, determine what level of work agreement is appropriate. If you choose to create a more formal written document (contract or project plan) you will probably want to send a first draft to the client for review and input. A more informal type of work agreement, such as a written summary in the form of a confirming memo or e-mail, can be used if desired.

Regardless of whether the work agreements you create are formal or informal, they need to be communicated to all who are either directly or indirectly involved, including other clients, team members, and subject matter experts. If you are making commitments on their behalf, it is important to include them in the process.

In addition, as part of your ongoing working relationship with all client groups, revisit the work agreement from time to time, test its assumptions, and make revisions. Many of our clients find that regular status reports serve as a valuable reminder of when it is time to revisit the work agreement.

The following is a sample work agreement for an internal project. It will give you an idea of format and content. The idea is to include all the important information, but keep it simple and easy to read.

Sample Work Agreement

Background

XYZ Department will double its employee population over the next twelve months and wishes to provide a hiring and selection training program to prepare managers to find and select the most qualified personnel. Karen Mason, department manager, has asked Chris Smith of the Corporate Training Center to identify a training program that can be customized to the needs of the department and implemented within 90 days.

Objectives
Select and implement a customized hiring and selection training program for twenty managers within XYZ Department.

Deliverables
Assessment of current hiring and selection skills of managers

Training program that meets the needs of managers and the department

Process Used to Meet Objectives
1. Conduct two focus groups with a cross section of managers to discuss their capabilities, needs, and concerns as related to locating and hiring new employees.
2. Present summary of focus groups' findings and recommendations to Karen Mason.
3. Identify training companies that offer selection and hiring courses.
4. Observe presentations of various training approaches. Review proposals from the vendors. Work with Karen Mason to select the course that best meets the needs of the department.
5. Review course materials with training vendor and identify areas of customization. Develop budget based on customization and implementation requirements.
6. Conduct initial course session with small group of managers to validate customization approaches. Revise as needed.
7. Offer training on open enrollment basis. However, the course will be mandatory before the end of the fiscal year.

Resources Required
Chris Smith will involve all appropriate managers within the department as needed for focus groups, input on customization, conducting initial session, and implementation over the next four months.

Focus groups will be held in department conference room.

Status Reporting
Chris Smith will update Karen Mason weekly.

Success Criteria
Within ten days of the managers' having completed the training course, Chris Smith will follow up with a cross-section of managers to determine the following:

Improvement in selection and hiring capabilities

Feedback on use of skills and techniques with applicants

Additional training, support, or coaching managers need

Team Work Agreements

Once you have drafted a work agreement with your primary client, you may also want to hold a work agreement discussion with others who will be involved, particularly team members. It is important that the team understand the background, current situation, and scope of the work. Team members' comfort with what is being asked of them will help ensure their commitment to the objectives and their roles.

During the team work agreement meeting, clarify *what* the team will be doing as well as *how* the team will work together. Strategically, this meeting is critical to you in managing the project or work assignment, so be prepared in your Consultative Roles as facilitator, influencer, and coach to help your team easily overcome obstacles and resolve any questions or conflicts. Sometimes the team discussion can be challenging, as people may have concerns or differing ideas or may be resistant.

> *"It is a fine thing to have ability, but the ability to discover the ability in others is the true test."*
> —Elbert Hubbard

Gerard Crum, senior associate at CB Commercial Real Estate, describes his positive experience with using a team work agreement: "At the time I went through The Consultative Approach workshop, I was grappling with how to win a piece of business. I pulled a team together and developed a team work agreement to define what each of us would be accountable for and how we would work together. At first, the aim was to get ourselves organized and be clear on compensation. The original work agreement was tailored toward getting the assignment. But later, when we got the business, it was updated to focus on how we would move forward working with the client. Getting all the issues out on the table early was critical to our success. It was just phenomenal, kind of like the stars and planets lining up! It all fell into place as we worked through the work agreement discussion."

Following is a list of topics to discuss in your team work agreement meeting. Once again, this is simply a starting place for you to use in creating a template of your own.

Team Work Agreement Topics

- *Team members' introductions, experience and expertise:* Each person's expertise and talents may be assumed or hidden. Have people share what they can contribute and what they want to learn from the experience.

- *Clarification of project goals:* Explain the client's business, strategies, and project goals as they are linked to the client's overall objectives. Provide an opportunity for clarification and discussion of the client's business.

- *Clarification of work relationships:* The discussion of how you want to work together should include such topics as roles, responsibilities, work style, communication strategy for the team and the client, areas of personal interest and disinterest, levels of involvement, hidden agendas, ground rules for working together, status reporting, invoicing process, assumptions each team member is operating under, and how conflict will be resolved. *How* you will work together is equally as important as what you will be doing.

- *Clarification of activities:* Your discussion about what is to be done may follow a traditional project-management approach, in which you decide on tasks, activities, milestones, resources, and contingency plans. Make sure these elements are linked with your decisions about how you will work together.

- *Confirmation and next steps:* Record your agreements and next steps. This document can be copied and sent to everyone on e-mail or kept on flipcharts to remind the team members how they are going to work together.

For the purposes of illustration, we have included a sample team work agreement. It does not take much time to create a comprehensive work agreement if you have a framework in mind when you start.

Sample Team Work Agreement

Team Members

Jerry, Sonya, and Ling (MIS)

Pam and Rashid (Marketing Department)

Background

The director of Marketing has requested a new network that would enable the department to work via the Internet/intranet with its public relations and marketing vendors. The network must meet the security requirements of the company and the needs of its vendors.

Objectives

Determine feasibility of internet/intranet network for the marketing department in working with outside vendors.

Make recommendations to directors of Marketing and MIS for network vendors, hardware, and software.

Deliverables

Summary report of feasibility study

Evaluation of network vendors and hardware and software considerations

Key Activities and Schedule

April 1: Jerry identifies networking consultants who have designed similar networks and user companies who have installed them.

April 15: Sonya, Pam, and Rashid identify needs of marketing department, public relations, and marketing vendors.

April 20: Ling identifies security issues with MIS director and determines limitations with the marketing department.

April 30: Team develops selection criteria for choosing networking vendor, hardware and software options.

May 15: Team meets with network vendors to review their processes for design, implementation, and maintenance of network.

May 30: Jerry, Sonya, and Ling complete first draft of feasibility study report.

June 10: Pam and Rashid review and give input to first draft.

June 15: Team presents study and network consultant vendor recommendations to Directors of Marketing and MIS.

Resources Required

One-half time for Jerry, Sonya

One-quarter time for Ling, Pam, and Rashid

Status Reporting

All members of team provide status once per week as to timeline, challenges, and progress.

Assumptions

Additional time for study may be needed based on new information discovered during the process.

The directors of Marketing and MIS will be available during this period of time for at least two hours per week for the purpose of giving input, answering questions and updates.

MIS standard operating procedures and interface requirements will be compatible with whatever we implement.

A vendor decision will be made by June 15, so that we can implement the network by September 1.

Budget

In addition to salaries of the team, budget for the study is estimated to be $10,000 for travel to user site demonstrations and meetings at vendor offices.

Steve Umphreys, vice president of Human Resources at International Network Services, emphasizes the importance of team work and team work agreements at his company: "We have found that our engineers will not be successful if we don't serve our clients in a team approach, as the business needs and solutions are too complex to do alone. Teams in our situation consist of those who are on site as well as the virtual team members across the country that can be called on for knowledge, expertise, and ideas on any given problem. This collaborative team approach is one of our competitive advantages, and using team work agreements is a key tool."

Creating a Work Agreement

1. Select a client or team with whom you want to clarify expectations, confirm roles and responsibilities, and document your collective agreement. It may be a client or team you are currently working with or one with whom you will be meeting in the near future to discuss a project or task.

2. Using the list of work agreement topics, outline your understanding of each area (as appropriate), based on what you know now. When it's completed, read through it and identify any areas about which you are not clear or for which you need more information.

3. Meet with your client or team and discuss those areas you have questions about. Also confirm that
   —Your client or team is clear about the project.
   —The expectations each of you has are defined.
   —Potential obstacles are identified and planned for.

4. Ask the client or team for feedback on creating the work agreement. What worked? What didn't?

CHAPTER HIGHLIGHTS

- Work agreements are documented in a way that corresponds to the complexity of the situation and the number of people involved. Remember, it is better to overcommunicate than to make too many assumptions.

- A work agreement discussion focuses not only on *what* you will be doing, but on *how* you would like to work with the client.

- Demonstrate all the Consultative Roles, particularly that of strategist, during your work agreement discussions. This will help the client to see you in the role of business partner rather than as just technical expert.

- Keep abreast of your client's business, industry trends, and strategies, and look for the hidden nuggets that will set you apart.

- Use work agreements successfully by following these general steps:

    —Key Activity 1: Understand the client's business and needs

    —Key Activity 2: Conduct the work agreement discussion

    —Key Activity 3: Develop and communicate the work agreement

- Develop your own personal work agreement template to use with all clients. Include key questions in a format that can be easily adapted to any situation.

- Remember to create a team work agreement with those who will be involved in the project.

CHAPTER EIGHT

STAYING ON COURSE

The heart of Phase 2 of the Consultative Process, defining key issues and solution ideas, is to "ask for directions"—to seek out information and insights beyond what the circle of people involved in creating the initial work agreement have to offer. This phase is important, whether you're embarking on a massive, long-term organizational project or simply implementing a straightforward assignment. Your goal is to deepen your level of expertise by gathering information and insights about what will produce an optimum result in implementation. To do this, you formally and informally assess the needs and issues of all client groups, uncover potential obstacles and detours, and translate your learnings into solution ideas.

> "Let us keep our mouths shut and our pens dry until we know the facts."
>
> —A. J. Carlson

Why is it often a challenge to stay on course? Because it's easy to get off track or possibly be on the wrong path in the first place. Remember the central role of feedback in the Consultative Process model? Sometimes it seems that the fewer people—and the less feedback—involved in a project, the easier things will be. Nothing could be further from the truth. When you're driving through unfamiliar country without a map,

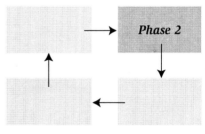

the best thing you can do is ask directions—early and often—and any project is to some extent uncharted territory. There are always new challenges, different people involved, changing circumstances. The important thing is not to proceed to implementation based on your own assumptions or limited information.

As an effective consultative partner, you cast your net widely during this phase. Your goal is to check in with every client group that can provide you with the input you need to implement your goal successfully. And by seeking a deeper understanding of key issues and considering new solution concepts, you will also create buy-in and commitment from everyone involved.

119

In this phase you will determine a strategy for giving all client groups the opportunity to provide feedback and direction on the issues that will affect them. For example, your financial clients will be interested in the budget implications of a decision. End user clients may express concern about how the program, system, or initiative will impact their day-to-day lives. Team members will want to share their insights about people, process, and management of certain situations. Your project may not produce optimum results unless you hear from all of these people.

RESULTS OR OPTIMUM RESULTS?

Participants in our workshops have often said that Phase 2 is a luxury they often can't afford. A constant driving force surrounds their work: the unrelenting pressure to produce results, results, results. This drive is natural and necessary to get work done. But the constant stress to "get it done" usually results in the loss of valuable insights and, therefore, less-than-optimum results. Those all-important results—the ones that get so much emphasis at evaluation time—are compromised because red flags weren't given attention, signs of resistance were ignored, or clients weren't asked for critical feedback. Your primary and financial clients, along with your own perceived sense of urgency, might lure you into skipping or breezing through Phase 2. Don't!

Every day, you have the opportunity to deepen your knowledge and insights about the best course to take in a given situation, the best strategy to use in working with a client, and the best way to leverage your expertise. It's true that you can't always do a thorough needs analysis or survey or gather all the information you need. But being consultative and striving to be seen as a business partner mean continuing to gain insights about all your client groups and constantly looking for opportunities to involve them in your work. During this phase, spend as much time and energy as the realities of your project timeline allow in defining key issues and expanding your information and insights.

Another reality of Phase 2 is that things are constantly changing. Senior management suddenly adds a different twist or new layer to the work. Your primary client gets transferred to another assignment, and her replacement wants you to use a different approach. Your project gets a lot of press within the company, and the pressure to complete it increases tenfold. You are constantly presented with situations and opportunities that require you to change course and evaluate options based on a new set of circumstances. Working consultatively requires flexibility and it requires judgment. When your insights tell you that the changed situation is pulling you down a path that will not produce an optimum result, listen to your intuition and take action. It will make the difference between producing results and producing optimum results.

THE BALANCE BETWEEN STRAIGHTFORWARD
AND MORE COMPLEX APPROACHES

How much time and energy can you afford to spend in Phase 2? Achieving your goals could be accomplished by a few quick phone calls to get input to validate your assumptions. On the other hand, you may need to commit to days of information gathering, observation, diagnosis, and problem identification. It all depends on the project, the players, and other factors that continue to evolve over the course of your project. Therefore the activities and time frame that you feel are critical for Phase 2 depend on where you see yourself in the straightforward-to-complex spectrum of approaches. In determining where your project falls on the spectrum, consider the following:

- How simple or complicated is the situation, project, or assignment?
- How many people are involved, affected by the results, or concerned about implementation issues?
- How visible is the work or expected end result?
- How political is the project, task, or assignment?
- What are your client groups' expectations about being involved and giving input?
- Do you need to strengthen the level of commitment from various client groups?
- What is the expected length of time of the project?

Using the preceding questions, you can assess the types of activities you strategically need to consider to get the most out of the time you invest in Phase 2.

THE CONSULTATIVE ROLES OF PHASE 2

In this chapter, you will consider what you need to do to gather feedback and ideas from others. In doing so you will have the opportunity to play all the consultative roles:

- *Problem solver*—getting to the root cause of issues and searching for solution options
- *Strategist*—linking future opportunities, business challenges, and long-term implications
- *Facilitator*—asking questions and making it easy for people to provide information and insights

- *Technical expert*—knowing what information and insights you need to explore with all client groups
- *Coach*—helping all your client groups to understand their roles in defining issues and brainstorming solutions
- *Influencer*—persuading client groups to share their feedback and concerns
- *Administrator*—organizing and managing the feedback process
- *Partner*—creating an open and trusting forum so that people will share honest opinions and needs

KEY ACTIVITIES FOR PHASE 2

Use these three key activities as a guide for achieving your goals during Phase 2 of the Consultative Process:

- Key Activity 1: Determine information and insight areas to explore with all client groups.
- Key Activity 2: Discuss key issues and brainstorm solution ideas with all client groups.
- Key Activity 3: Discuss key issues and solution ideas with the primary client.

Key Activity 1: Determine Information and Insight Areas to Explore with All Client Groups

You have already started uncovering important information on areas to explore with client groups. In your work agreement discussions you reviewed not only how you and the primary client will work together but also how you will go about getting input and agreement from various client groups: end users, subject matter experts, team members, financial stakeholders, and external customers.

At this stage of the game, you want to develop a strategy for gathering information and insights. You may also want to plan or review your strategies with your primary client or team. The following are some areas to consider when organizing your Phase 2 game plan:

- Which client groups can provide additional information and insights you can learn from?
- What are the most appropriate methods of information gathering (focus groups, face-to-face interviews, surveys)?
- What are the best ways to contact people to make appointments, prepare them for the discussion or survey, and explain a context for what is happening?

- When selecting which individuals or groups to talk to, consider
  —Who can provide information, perceptions, ideas, history, or similar experiences
  —Which clients or groups are politically important to talk with
  —Who might have concerns or be resistant and therefore need to be brought into the process early
  —Which people are viewed as champions within the organization
  —Which clients or groups that you have selected represent different levels within the organization, geographic or cultural perspectives, and needs and areas of expertise

Aligning Organizational, Operational, and Individual Areas. To help you plan a comprehensive information-gathering strategy, we suggest a framework for examining factors across organizational, operational, and individual areas, as shown in the graphic. As an illustration, Table 8.1 lists the technical expertise of five consultants, the outcomes they have been asked to deliver, and which area they might focus their attention on.

In each of these examples, the person with the expertise is being asked to focus on a single organizational, operational, or individual issue; however, to be effective, each person needs to consider the interrelationship among

Table 8.1 Areas of Focus.

Technical Expertise	Outcome	Area of Focus
Training or Learning Consultant	Improve the way in which people work as a team	Individual
Systems Engineer	Establish a secure network for the company	Operational
Commercial Real Estate Broker	Find a building with 10,000 square feet in the city to be used for data processing	Operational
Strategic Planner	Develop the overall strategy for a new product	Organizational
Product Development Manager	Determine new process for developing products that includes sales, marketing, technical consultants, manufacturing, and production	Operational

all three areas. Individuals possess differing skill and motivational levels. Operational processes, procedures, technical systems, and practices support individuals and their work. Organizational vision, leadership, goals, objectives, strategies, style, and culture guide it all.

The alignment of these areas is critical for success, no matter how small or large your project or task. Most project and initiative failures are caused by a lack of alignment among these three elements. Not considering the impact these factors have on each other—and not planning for it—leads to big problems during implementation.

 Donald McKinney, chair and CEO of International Network Services, describes how the three factors affect his company's business: "When we started International Network Services, we played the role of the dentist. We probed to find the pain, and we went from tooth to tooth. The client was in pain, so cost was less of a concern than time. 'Get it fixed fast' was the goal. Now our goal is to build a network of strategic importance and do that with an experience base that is exploding. This requires us to include organizational, operational, and individual factors."

Organizational Factors. In reviewing organizational factors, you should determine whether there are discrepancies between the vision, the goals, and the culture of the company or unit. Also strive to understand the nature of the business environment and the impact of anticipated changes. These factors are especially important in understanding management's priorities, philosophies, and plans. Overall, you are assessing the organization's readiness for your potential recommendations. Organizational factors include the following:

- Vision, goals, objectives, and strategies
- Culture, style, politics, and human resource philosophy
- Business trends, financial picture, business plans, life cycle of products, and competition
- Communication and information management
- Change-management strategies

To help you get started in planning your questioning strategy for Key Activity 1, use the following list of sample questions on organizational factors. As you read through the list, consider how you will adapt the questions to the strategic issues facing your own clients.

- How does this project relate to the vision and goals of the organization?
- What are the client's specific objectives, expected outcomes, and concerns for this project?
- What is the company's style or culture, and how does it affect the success of the initiative?
- Does the human resource philosophy support the project goals?
- What growth is anticipated, and how will it affect the decisions made now and in the future?
- What are management's, employees', and customers' perceptions of the current situation?
- How are the issues being managed? What is causing or maintaining the problem?
- What solution ideas do employees and management have?
- What is the readiness level of the different client groups being affected?
- Who in the organization/group will have difficulty with this approach?
- How does information get communicated to people?

Operational Factors. When considering operational factors, you will want to examine any processes, practices, and systems that are already in place and whether they will support or hinder the changes you may propose.

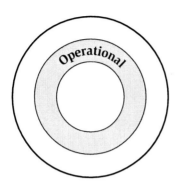

Potential changes in routines and systems can impact performance either positively or negatively and will require transition plans. Overall, you need to assess whether or not the organization's infrastructure will support your potential recommendations. Operational factors include the following:

- Systems, processes, practices, and distribution of information
- Success measures and quality improvement
- Performance-management systems
- Change-management transition plans

To develop your questioning strategy for operational factors, consider the following examples:

- Which policies, processes, procedures, and routines are helping you and the client to meet the goal? Which ones are hindering you?
- Which operations might be outsourced? How does this affect the project?
- Which technical systems are critical to the initiative? What percentage of improvements or changes need to be made based on the desired outcomes?
- What impact will there be on software/hardware systems and other job tools?
- Which support systems are critical to the project?
- In terms of best use of technical systems and processes, what does success look like?
- Which management systems are in place (or not in place) that are critical to the project's success?
- Do the performance systems need to be adjusted to support and complement the change? If so, how?
- Are there plans for involving people in the systems changes?
- What resistance do you expect from people?
- Have you been successful in managing similar changes before? If so, what did you do?

Individual Factors. In your focus on individual issues, look at the factors that help or hinder people in the performance of their jobs. Clarity on the attitudes, skill levels, willingness to adopt changes, and development needs of people will contribute to the quality of the outcome you produce. These factors are especially important in understanding the world of end user client groups and any gaps in their understanding or performance. Overall, you are assessing whether or not individuals have the willingness and ability to adopt and implement the changes you may recommend. Individual factors include the following:

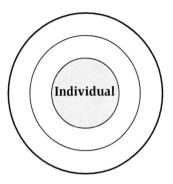

- Skills, knowledge, and sharing of information
- Motivation, attitude, and morale
- Performance enhancement and continuous learning
- Change and transition support

Suggestions for questions you can ask to explore individual factors follow. You will want to adjust these questions to correspond to the types of job functions that will be affected by the results of your project and the changes that will occur.

- What performance results do you expect?
- Which competencies are required for this group of people as related to the business goals to be achieved?
- What are the best practices for specific people or positions as related to the business goals to be achieved?
- In your opinion, what is getting in the way of people employing best practices?
- Is the performance management system aligned with the competencies required and best practices?
- What is the level of motivation and willingness to embrace the project?
- What is getting in the way of people embracing the project?
- Have people who will be affected been part of the process of deciding *how* to work differently?
- Is a transition plan in place for helping people through the changes?
- Are there linkages between what people are being asked to do and how their actions are being reinforced and rewarded?

Known and Unknown Problems and Opportunities. In exploring the organizational, operational, and individual factors in Phase 2, your goal is to learn more about the issues you are aware of and identify unknown or suspected problems or opportunities. *Known* problems and opportunities are the issues you have identified and will explore further. *Unknown* problems and opportunities are issues that you currently are unaware of and need to identify as well as those areas you suspect might be a factor and want to pursue. Some important known and unknown problems are the organizational, operational, and individual "red flag" insights you get about situations and people. The red flags might include people's concerns and needs or lack of commitment from a key player. In both cases you need a strategy for overcoming or minimizing the impact of these issues.

> "Anything that interferes with individual progress ultimately will retard group progress."
>
> —George Houston

The degree to which you delve into known and unknown issues may be a function of how straightforward or compound your data-gathering needs are. Another factor is how comfortable your primary client is with your pursuing certain issues. For example, if your client sees you as a technical expert, he or she may expect you to know the answer to a problem or to provide ideas for only the technical issues. But one major distinction between being a technical expert and a business partner is that a partner identifies challenges, develops potential solutions, and has a broader and more strategic context for his or her work.

> "We are confronted with insurmountable opportunities."
>
> —Walt Kelly

You may need to influence your client's thinking to allow more time for and commitment to information gathering if your expertise and intuition tell you to do so. As John Drew, president and COO of International Network Services, puts it, "Many clients don't know what they don't know until they get in the middle of it."

Table 8.2 was adapted from a model used at Arthur Andersen Performance and Learning. It shows the relationship between known and unknown or suspected problems, your role in addressing those problems, and—depending on the approach you use—how your clients perceive you.

Your goal is to look for the known and unknown or suspected problems, linkages, and misalignments that exist or may arise. Using your knowledge about organizational, operational, and individual issues, you can then come forward with solution ideas. Don't be afraid to be diligent about confirming known issues or uncovering unknown ones. In doing this you may be going outside your own areas of expertise or your comfort level, but by sharing your insights and concerns about possible obstacles or signs of misalignment, you add value to the process and avoid problems down the road.

Table 8.2. Known and Unknown Problems and Opportunities.

Client	You	Client's Perception of You
Has known problem	Have known solution	Technical Expert
Has unknown or suspected problem	Have known solution	Technical Expert Problem Solver
Has known problem	Have expertise and knowledge of the business to develop solution and implement	Consultant
Has unknown or suspected problem	Have expertise and knowledge of the business to develop solution and implement	Business Partner

Tips for Determining Information and Insight Areas

- Plan appropriate questions for discussion with your various client groups. Explore how your clients will be impacted by your project or initiative and seek to understand their related objectives or concerns.
- Expand the topics of your questioning to uncover possible areas that are not yet known to the client.
- Check the alignment of organizational, operational, and individual issues in terms of what will produce an optimum result. Consider
  —How this project, task, or assignment will support the organization's overall strategy
  —What impact this project, task, or assignment will have on the current operations and processes
  —What impact this project, task, or assignment will have on individuals' abilities and willingness to do their jobs
- Plan how you will contact the client groups from whom you will be gaining information and insights.
- Develop your own library of questions that you can ask different client groups.

Identifying the Change and Transition-Management Issues. Your work world is probably changing faster and faster. Structures, processes, and directions are all changing, and it is the things that change that require people to make adjustments. You and your clients must constantly adapt to situations over which you have no control. This requires creativity, resiliency, and a willingness to work with a daily dose of ambiguity. As a consultative business partner, you must focus both on the management of changing structures, processes, and procedures and on the management of people making the transitions.

One aspect of Phase 2 of the Consultative Process is understanding the dynamics of change and its impact on your client groups. People handle change in various ways, at different paces. If you can determine your client groups' issues, motivations, and rewards, you will be able to better guide them through this uncharted territory.

William Bridges, author of a series of books on transition management, uses a three-stage model that is extremely useful in helping people progressively adapt to change. He identifies the three phases as Ending, Losing, Letting Go; The Neutral Zone; and The New Beginning. His point is that incorporating a change and transition plan into your Phase 2 solution idea improves your chances of success.

Ending of the Old Way. In beginning a transition, people start with an ending of the old way. As Bridges points out, rituals were created to help people let go and deal with the sense of loss we face. Graduation from school is called the commencement ceremony, which focuses on a new beginning or transition from student to working professional. Weddings, funerals, retirement dinners, celebrations, and ceremonies of all kinds help us end the old ways and begin anew. In work, this same premise is applicable. As change is thrust upon you and your clients, find rituals to let go of old ways and begin the next step forward.

Laura Penland, vice president of Science Applications International Corporation (SAIC), discusses the value of such a symbolic step: "Employees of SAIC, an employee-owned company, have a great deal of pride in the company name. The company has a long history, especially in the defense industry, as a superb system integrator. As a new group, our mission was to develop the commercial health care market. Our initial agreement with one client was to work at the client's facilities in order to truly partner and work as a team.

"Within the first three months, both sides could see that we had not made the transition as well as we had hoped. At this point, the client asked us to wear the client's company badges instead of ours in order to close the "us-versus-them" gap. In the meeting in which we announced this, the SAIC employees were at first appalled at the request. Then they began to recognize the value in being viewed as a member of the client's company. This ritual was the beginning of a true partnering relationship with the client."

Managing Neutral Zone Discomfort. Bridges describes the *neutral zone* as an interim phase of awkwardness in which both creativity and chaos exist. Think of any major change you have experienced—buying a home, starting a new job, getting married, taking a vacation, having a house guest, buying a new car. Even though you may have been excited about the change, you may also have experienced an awkward feeling of not being used to it yet. In organizations, this is usually the time when confusion and resistance reign. Bridges suggests that one key to managing neutral zone discomfort is to create temporary systems as a way of helping people transition and stay productive while the change is being implemented.

> "Habit is habit, and not to be flung out of the window by any man, but coaxed downstairs a step at a time"
>
> —Mark Twain

A facilities manager in one of our workshops related this anecdote about using such interim solutions: "We were moving our offices and, as we all know, moving is one of the most stressful experiences people can have. Even though a team of professional movers was moving us over a weekend, people still had to pack and unpack their spaces. We knew that this was going to be incredibly disruptive, and we wanted to get everybody up and running as quickly as possible. We created a task force of people from each floor to help develop a variety of temporary systems—such as hotlines, room monitors, technical teams for computers and phones, floating cellular phones, and food—in order to ensure that people's productivity did not drop as a result of the move. We were back in business by the end of the day on Monday, which was a miracle, and people were not stressed out at all. In fact we had a great time."

Beginning the Change. Adoption of change can be easy for some and extremely difficult for others. In Phase 2, look for areas of potential difficulty as people move toward the new beginning. You may have to deal with the following:

- Expectations of those (especially senior management) who had the vision for the change, who will be there long before anyone else, and who will wonder why things are taking so long

- Resistance from those who move through the transition more slowly, hanging on to the old way and making "noise" in the system

- Confusion, uncertainty, and a wait-and-see attitude

- Loss of productivity, depression, and low morale

Key Activity 2: Discuss Key Issues and Brainstorm Solution Ideas with All Client Groups

Key Activity 1 helped you focus on defining which organizational, operational, and individual factors you wanted to explore further. Now that you are clear on what you want to know, it is time to move to the next step: discussing key issues and brainstorming solution ideas with all client groups. During this stage of Phase 2, you are using your ability to "peel the onion," discuss ideas, check out assumptions, brainstorm solutions, and define what success looks like to your client.

"Necessity of action takes away the fear of the act."

—Quarles

Before you begin discussing key issues with your clients be sure you do the following:

- Review with your primary client or team the list of individuals and groups from whom you intend to get input.

- Develop questions to cover the spectrum of organizational, operational, and individual issues you wish to explore.

- Determine the formal and informal methods you will use with individuals and groups to gather information and insights—phone, face-to-face interviews, focus groups, surveys.

- Establish a plan for keeping your primary client or team in the loop as you begin the information-gathering process. Your job will be much easier in the long run if you schedule the few minutes required for updates. Determine the frequency and the best vehicles for updates (phone, voice mail, face-to-face conversation, e-mail, status reports) well ahead of time.

Ways to Gather Information and Insights. When we say *discuss key issues* we use the word *discuss* in the broadest sense. There are many effective ways to collect information, from objective survey research to informal chats around the water cooler. In choosing a method, your key considerations need to be the amount of time available and the type of insights you want to gain.

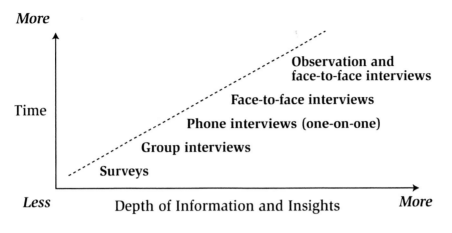

Figure 8.1. Ways to Gather Information and Insights.

Figure 8.1 shows several options for gathering information and insights depending on your time frame and the depth of information and insights you wish to acquire.

A combination of strategies can also be very effective. For example, if you conduct a broad survey, follow it up with more in-depth interviews. Conduct focus groups with people who represent a majority population, such as end users. One-on-one interviews work best in cases when you need privacy to encourage someone to open up and reveal deeper thoughts and feelings. Senior management, for example, is a group best interviewed one-on-one.

You may also wonder how many people you need to contact. We use two criteria to determine the answer. First, who can give you the best and most honest insights? Ask your coach, primary client, and team members to suggest people and approaches that will give you the greatest "bang for the buck" within the allotted time. Second, determine who you can't afford to omit because you need their support and commitment. Interviews with these people will help you see where they stand and allow you to clarify—or even influence—their attitudes.

Phone Interviews. What do you do when you need good information but just don't have time to interview lots of people? When deadlines are tight, you are already overworked, and you have limited resources, pick up the phone! Using the phone saves time and money and, if done well, can produce mountains of key information. Although you don't get the important nonverbal clues you would in a face-to-face discussion, the phone is still a highly effective information-gathering tool.

We advocate conducting phone interviews as a starting point. If after the phone call you need more time with the person, schedule a meeting. Phone appointments generally take less time than face-to-face interviews. Depending on the topics, thirty to forty-five minutes is usually enough.

Tips for Phone Interviews

1. Plan the interview well. Set up a phone appointment for the interview and confirm the time and topics you will be discussing. If you send an agenda ahead of time, the interviewee will be better prepared, and you will the use time more effectively.

2. Start the conversation by reviewing the purpose of the call and the time available.

3. Approximately halfway through the interview, ask questions that take the conversation to a deeper level, such as

   —Do you have any other concerns, issues, or ideas I should know about regarding this situation?

   —If you wanted to make sure one thing happened to make this project successful, what would it be?

   —How will you know that we have been successful? What would success look like to you?

4. Find shorthand ways to capture the person's comments and your insights that do not distract either you or the person being interviewed. If you are a fast typist you can type into a computer as people speak. If that is distracting, then consider tape recording for later reference. If you use either of these methods, be sure to ask the person's permission to take notes in that manner.

5. Leave people feeling that their ideas are valuable and will be used in conjunction with all the other information you gather. Most importantly, people need to finish the conversation feeling hopeful and excited about the possible outcomes and about being part of the process. End the conversation by thanking the person for taking the time to speak with you, and ask the person to call you if he or she thinks of anything else (making sure to give your own telephone number).

Other Methods to Collect Information and Insights. Many situations will require face-to-face meetings, group interviews, surveys, or visual observations of people or processes. And of course there are trade-offs associated with each approach. Table 8.3 summarizes some thoughts about the benefits and drawbacks of various information-gathering methods.

"You can observe a lot by just watching."
—Yogi Berra

Table 8.3. Benefits and Drawbacks
of Information-Gathering Methods.

Method	Benefits	Drawbacks
Observation in the workplace	• Provides insights that cannot be obtained any other way • Provides opportunity to observe interactions, processes, work flow, and obstacles • Gives you a firsthand impression rather than having to rely on someone else's interpretation	• Time-consuming • Getting permission to observe others in action may be difficult • Your presence may make people distracted or self-conscious and thus change the way things are normally done
Face-to-face interviews	• Easier to discuss sensitive or confidential information • More likely to get buy-in to project, process, and ideas • More intimate setting builds a greater level of trust • Able to pick up on body language and nonverbal clues • Better able to collect anecdotes, examples, and stories	• Time-consuming if you are interviewing many people • If travel is involved, can add to time required • Scheduling can be difficult. If available, use administrative support to coordinate scheduling.
Phone interviews	• Easy to schedule • Minimal costs and time • Can do many of them in a short period of time • Will be more prepared with precise questions (this is a good habit to get into) • Can record in real time by computer or tape	• Have to work harder at building rapport • More likely for you and client to be distracted or interrrupted • Easy to get sloppy in preparing for the meeting • Miss nonverbal clues to develop PLOT

Table 8.3. Benefits and Drawbacks
of Information-Gathering Methods (*continued*).

Method	Benefits	Drawbacks
Group Interviews	• Access to cross section of larger populations • Saves time • Get group response and input (don't run the risk of relying on one person's opinion or idea) • Can confirm or clarify results from surveys or face-to-face interviews	• Tend to get general concerns rather than specific ones • Requires excellent facilitation skills to manage the discussion and get good information • Difficult to bring up political or sensitive information in a group setting
Surveys	• Can get information from large groups of people • Information can be used to analyze statistical significance	• Need at least two hours for group of 6 to 12 people • Need second person to take notes if you are not using a tape recorder • Survey has to be well designed to get good information • No opportunity to "peel the onion" to find out why respondents answered the way they did • Response may be low and therefore insignificant

Think Ahead

Regardless of the methods you choose, think ahead about the best ways to capture information and insights so that the material is useful at a later time to you, your primary client, and your team. For example:

- If you tape-record interviews, be sure to ask permission first, especially if you want to share the tapes with other team members. Depending upon the need and your budget, tapes can also be transcribed. Even though you may be taping the interview, take notes during the interview to outline key points in the conversation so that when you listen to the tape later, you have a guide for locating the noteworthy parts of the conversation.

- During group interviews, use a second person as a recorder to take notes on key points of the discussion. Make sure that you have an agreement on the recorder's role and whether he or she is only to take notes or may also ask questions to clarify points captured.

- If members of your team are each doing interviews that will be compiled later, design a collective questioning strategy and agree on how the input will be summarized. Doing this up front is essential. Otherwise you will probably have to figure out later how to organize and sum up a mass of disparate data—a messy and time-consuming job. Check in periodically to determine if your information-gathering and compilation strategies are on target and make any necessary adjustments.

- If you conduct a survey that someone helps you to design, make sure that person knows how the information is to be used. If there is a specific report format you want, design the questionnaire so that responses fit easily into that format.

- If you are focusing on a specific technical area—such as performance issues, process improvement, or technological change—we suggest you review some of the specialty books on gathering data for those subjects. (See the Resources section at the end of the book for suggestions.)

Don't ignore the impact your project may have on your client's customers. Determine which, if any, client groups may want to be involved before, during, or after you make any customer contact.

Following are some topics you may want to discuss with your client's customers to better understand your project's possible impact on their situation or their attitudes toward your client, the group, or the organization.

> *"You can handle people more successfully by enlisting their feelings than by convincing their reason."*
>
> —Paul Parker

- What benefits, results, or effect do you anticipate from the expected change (process, spending, use of technology, expectations of service performance)?

- What additional information, knowledge, or skill do you need to make an easy transition?

- What inconveniences might you experience, and how could those be offset?

During Key Activities 1 and 2, look for ways to include your primary client in the planning and execution of information-gathering activities. Having the primary client work with you on the front end will ensure that he or she understands the rationale for what you are asking and who you are talking to. You may want your primary client to accompany you when you conduct certain interviews so that he or she will see the interaction firsthand and gain insights from the experience. Your primary client may want to participate for professional growth or political reasons or just out of curiosity. If your client is hesitant about participating, extend the invitation by sharing an Expertise Statement about how the client's participation is relevant to the desired outcomes.

Nancy Raymond, a performance consultant at Bank of America, tells the following story about the necessity of involving the primary client: "I was called in to manage the training design for a new software application. We were faced with several challenges. We were brought in late in the process, and the client kept getting more and more people involved as we developed the training. Plus we were working from opposing points of view, in that the training team felt that the application was complicated, but the client felt that it was easy to use and did not require in-depth training. During a meeting I finally realized that the client was under pressure to deliver an easy-to-use system, and he was concerned that wasn't going to happen. Once I realized that, we took a different approach. We listened to his concerns and found a way to compromise between bare bones and comprehensive training. We are still working on it, but the turning point was understanding the pressure he was under."

Once you've made the decision to involve your primary client in information-gathering activities, it's important to plan carefully how to go about it. It needs to be done very judiciously. First, consider the primary client's PLOT and consider how he or she can best be of value to you. If your PLOT observations suggest that this person is domineering or opinionated, or has difficulty listening, then it's probably not a good idea to have the client attend interviews—especially group interviews. Second, factor in both how the person is perceived and his or her level in the organization. If your primary client is either a higher-level manager or not well perceived by others, people may be reluctant to share their honest opinions and frames of reference. Find ways to use your primary client to your advantage during this phase. If he or she invests time now, then Phases 3 and 4 of the Consultative Process will go much easier.

Key Activity 3: Discuss Key Issues and Solution Ideas with the Primary Client

Once you have gathered your information, you need to summarize and analyze it. Of course, the process is not necessarily as linear as the preceding statement sounds. Information gathering is an ongoing process, and it takes many forms throughout the course of a project. As you collect information, formally and informally, you need to review it periodically and incorporate it into the larger picture. You also need periodically to assess your progress and present that progress to your clients.

Reviewing the Information You Have Collected. Periodically, you will want to review information, insights, assumptions, and concerns and test out or presell solution ideas with your primary client. One effective way to keep your primary client informed is what we call a "yellow pad review," which can be used throughout the project. For a yellow pad review, you jot down key observations, themes, and high-level summaries. Then walk through the list with your client as a progress check. This process is usually not time-consuming, and it allows you to cover critical updates, minimize surprises, and get coaching on strategies, next steps, and assumptions going forward. In this review with your primary client, consider the following as agenda topics:

- Does the 80/20 rule apply, and if so how? (The 80/20 rule holds that 80 percent of the problems come from 20 percent of the customers, processes, people, and so on.)
- Does the information reflect a root cause of a problem or just a symptom?
- What will happen if the problem is ignored?
- Is there a misalignment that needs to be dealt with immediately, or can it wait?
- Does what you are learning accurately measure the success of the project or initiative?
- Are there additional people that should be interviewed?

- Are all the client groups ready and committed to the change? If not, what is missing? What will help them get ready?

Conducting a Readiness Assessment. Once you have synthesized the information and insights, consider conducting a readiness assessment. This is a tool you can use to facilitate meaningful dialogue with team members, the primary client, and other critical client groups about the readiness for change in the organizational, operational, and individual areas. Readiness issues include the elements that must be in place for implementation to be successful. The readiness assessment itself is a discussion guide tailored to fit the specific situation and your learnings from gathering information. It provides an opportunity to develop solutions ideas with your team and primary client as appropriate. The following are some of the possible outcomes of using a readiness assessment.

- You identify readiness issues facing different client groups.
- You develop strategies for influencing others, facilitating discussion, and removing obstacles.
- You plan actions to help client groups through the neutral zone.
- You integrate your insights into the best way to build trust and commitment with all client groups.

Here are the steps in completing a readiness assessment:

1. Draw the readiness assessment on a flipchart so that everyone can see the grid. Clarify the vision and goals and define the scope of the project or assignment to ensure that everyone is operating under the same assumptions.

2. List all client groups that are affected by the project. Cluster client groups if necessary, but you may want to assess some clients individually. For example, a financial client might be assessed individually because of his or her importance to the project. Other clients may be grouped by management level, region, or function or into large categories such as employees or end users.

3. Select the readiness categories that are most important to the success of the project or assignment. We have included organizational, operational, and individual categories and key factors within each to help you identify misalignments.

4. Ask each person to rate the level of readiness for each client group or individual listed. Use a scale of 1 to 5, where 1 indicates a low level of readiness and 5 indicates a high level. For some categories, "not applicable" (N/A) may be appropriate.

Readiness Assessment

Project Scope _____

Project Vision or Goal _____

Rate your clients based on your sense of their level of readiness. Use a 1 to 5 scale:
1 is not ready; 5 is ready and raring to go. This assessment will give you a "big picture"
of your clients' level of readiness.

Clients*	Organizational		Operational		Individual	
	Vision/ Goals	Style/ Culture	Systems/ Processes	Management Practices	Skills	Motivation & Attitude

*These can be specific individuals or groups of clients such as senior management, middle managers, staff, and so on.

5.   Encourage discussion as everyone shares their ratings with the group. Completing a readiness assessment is not an exact science. Its value is not in the numbers but in the discussion of different insights and opinions and the subsequent collective learnings. So in facilitating the discussion, be prepared to handle disagreements and to encourage many ideas and solutions. You might use the following questions to guide the discussion:

- Are the vision and goals clearly understood and bought into by management and employees?
- Does this project fit the style and culture of the organization?
- Are the systems and processes that are necessary for each client group in place to enable this initiative to be successful?
- Does the client in question have the mangement practices in place as required in this project?
- How would you rate the specific clients' current skill levels versus what is needed for them to do their jobs as required in this project or initiative?
- What is the attitude and level of motivation for each client group as related to the success of the project?

6.   After the discussion, review the assessment and circle ratings of 3 or lower. The areas that need attention become quite obvious.

7.   As time allows, discuss possible solution ideas for getting people and things ready. You will use this information in Phases 3 and 4.

Making the Invisible Visible. One of the greatest services you can provide to your clients is to help them "make the invisible visible." Many assignments or projects are implemented behind the scenes. Therefore, people not directly involved often wonder, What are they doing? What are they spending money on? What results are they showing? You will minimize resistance if you work consultatively by helping your client groups define and document readiness in their plans and status reports.

Phase 2 represents your opportunity to deepen and broaden the information and insights that will help you sell, plan, and implement your recommendations successfully. Often forces within your work environment will encourage you to skip this phase or do only the minimum, in order to save time and money. Pay attention to your intuition and what you have learned from experience about red flags, obstacles, and success factors in your implementation efforts and influence your team and primary client to invest the time in this phase.

CHAPTER HIGHLIGHTS

- Develop a strategy for gathering information and insights and plan or review these strategies with your primary client or team. Consider the following areas when organizing your Phase 2 game plan:

    —Which client groups can provide information and insights you can learn from?

    —What are the most appropriate methods of information gathering (focus groups, face-to-face interviews, surveys)?

    —What are the best ways of contacting people to make appointments, prepare them for the discussion or survey, and explain a context for what is happening?

- The alignment of organizational, operational, and individual factors is critical for success, no matter how small or large your project or task. Not considering the impact these factors have on each other and not planning for it accordingly leads to big problems during implementation.

- Your goal is to learn more about the known issues and to identify any unknown or suspected problems or opportunities.

- As a consultative business partner, it is important to focus on both the management of changing *things*—structure, processes, and procedures—and the management of the *people* making the transitions.

- Use your ability to "peel the onion," discuss ideas, check out assumptions, brainstorm solution ideas, and define what success looks like to your client groups.

- In selecting the best information-gathering methods, weigh the amount of time and budget available against the type of insights you want to gain.

- Find ways to involve your primary client during this phase to develop his or her insights as well.

- Review information, insights, assumptions, and concerns and test out or presell solution ideas with your primary client.

- Conduct a readiness assessment with your team.

- Help your clients to "make the invisible visible."

CHAPTER NINE

WHERE THE RUBBER MEETS THE ROAD

As you begin this chapter on Phase 3, gaining commitment to your recommendations, think about what you have accomplished by using the Consultative Process to this point: you have demonstrated your value by playing all the Consultative Roles. You have created a mutual agreement for the project or assignment. You have investigated your client's situation and business. You have gathered information and gained insights from various client groups. Ideally, all that you have invested thus far in focus, time, and energy will pay off when your primary and financial clients commit to your recommendations.

Much of what you have learned in earlier chapters of this book will help you in this phase. Using PLOT will help you factor in the personality, language, opinion/frame of reference, and task approach of those with whom you will be reviewing your recommendations. Expertise Statements will help you share an insight, illustrate a point, or give a rationale. The Managing Client Interactions model will help you plan and facilitate the recommendations discussion.

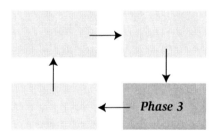

You have a critical next step ahead of you: gaining the commitment to proceed to implementation. That's why, strategically speaking, Phase 3 is the point in the Consultative Process when "the rubber meets the road."

BUILDING TRUST AND COMMITMENT

In reviewing aspects of Phase 3 that are critical to your success, we want to start with the very foundation of your partnering relationship—the level of trust and commitment. Simply put, a *commitment* is a pledge or promise to take an action in the future. Trust is the faith you put in people to make and keep commitments. Up to this point in the Consultative Process you have asked your primary client to make commitments, and he or she has trusted that your requests, recommendations, and judgment were on target. You have been laying the foundation of trust and commitment as you asked your client to create a work agreement, introduce you to people, let you interview different client groups, give you feedback, and help to solve problems.

Think about the clues you've observed that help you gauge your client's level of trust and commitment up until now. Have this client's commitments been easy or difficult to obtain? Have you gotten this person's time and the focus you needed to keep things moving ahead? Has the client been involved in the process up until this point? If so, what impressions have been made and what opinions have been formed? If not, what history, background, and perspective do you need to share to help position your recommendations and the reasoning behind them? How, in general, during this phase will you continue to build the trust and commitment that will get you one step closer to implementation?

"All business proceeds on beliefs, or judgments of probabilities, and not on certainties."

—Charles Eliot

THE CONSULTATIVE ROLES YOU PLAY IN PHASE 3

The core of Phase 3 is to make recommendations based on the information and insights you gathered in Phase 2 and to get commitment to what will be implemented in Phase 4. In doing so, your focus is on building trust and commitment, demonstrating flexibility, and keeping the process moving. The following are aspects of the Consultative Roles that will probably be required in Phase 3:

- *Problem solver*—addressing obstacles and concerns

- *Strategist*—tying recommendations to project and business objectives and goals

- *Facilitator*—directing recommendation discussions so that options and issues are surfaced and explored

- *Technical expert*—sharing information and insights learned from all client groups

- *Coach*—assisting clients in the analysis of options and trade-offs

- *Influencer*—persuading the client to consider the recommendations and options

- *Administrator*—preparing and organizing the presentation, interaction, or report

- *Partner*—demonstrating flexibility and openness to ideas and input

KEY ACTIVITIES FOR PHASE 3

Phase 3 includes the following three activities:

- Key Activity 1: Prepare for recommendations discussion
- Key Activity 2: Discuss information, insights, and recommendations
- Key Activity 3: Gain agreement on next steps

Key Activity 1: Prepare for Recommendations Discussion

This activity involves planning how you will present and sell your recommendations in the most compelling way and planning for the interaction, taking into account the people you will be meeting with. We have provided suggestions, tips, and strategies for planning the most effective ways to present your ideas, respond to questions, and be perceived as adding value.

Based on the nature of your project or initiative, determine how you can present your ideas to make an impact on people. If your recommendations are relatively straightforward, then Phase 3 may be just a formality. However, if gaining commitment to your recommendations requires the blessing of a variety of people and will occur in a formal setting, then preparing a presentation strategy is critical. Either way, you must plan what to say and how to say it.

> *"Successful selling is 90 percent preparation and 10 percent presentation."*
>
> —Bertrand Canfield

The following are some questions to consider when developing recommendations and options to present to your client:

- What commitment is required, and does it match the client's current level of commitment?
- Is there a visible champion in the organization who will spearhead this effort?
- What degree of influence or control does the client have in implementing the recommendations?
- Is there a visible link between the recommendation and the organization's business issues, strategies, and goals?
- How does each recommendation match up with the organizational culture (risk taking, conservative, technologically ahead or behind)?
- Is the level of readiness part of the recommendations?

Involve Your Primary Client. In Chapter Eight we mentioned the importance of involving your primary client in discussing and considering solution ideas. Involving your client is an opportunity to presell ideas and identify those areas that will be of concern. At this stage, Phase 3, you may want your primary client to play a role in formulating recommendations and influencing others to buy into the ideas (if, that is, the client is credible within the organization and in a position to influence others). This can be a blockbuster strategy, but remember that it also may mean that you have to give up the limelight, get your ego out of the way, and trust that—with your coaching—the client will be successful.

Use Stories, Analogies, and Dramatic Demonstrations. A very powerful method of communicating when you ask people to make a commitment is to use stories, analogies, and demonstrations to make your point. Examples, anecdotes, and dramatic points are often what stick in people's minds when someone has presented ideas. When you make your recommendations, your clients will be very interested in your observations of why people said what they did, why people have the concerns they do, and what led to the insights you have shared.

> *"Any fact is better established by two or three good testimonies than by a thousand arguments."*
>
> —Emmons

The following story illustrates the impact of a dramatic demonstration. Jean Roux, global strategies and health consultant at Levi Strauss, was responsible for developing an HIV/AIDS awareness program within the Asia Pacific division for employees, consumers, and the community. At a managers' meeting, he was to present his key learnings to date and ask for commitment to implement the program. He was scheduled to present right after lunch and was ready with an armful of data and overheads. As he walked to the podium, he noticed that everyone's eyes were heavy, and they were slouched in their chairs. So to wake them up, Roux decided to take a risk. He looked at the group of senior managers and said, "How many of you have had sex in the past year?" Everyone immediately looked up in utter surprise. Then he went on to ask, "How many of you have had sex with someone other than your primary partner?"

When uncomfortable laughter broke out in the room, he seized the moment by continuing to link the business need to his recommendations: "HIV infection is increasing rapidly in this region. I want you to understand the implications on the business and our communities. In fact, approximately 40 million people in Asia Pacific will be infected with HIV by the year 2000, unless we intervene dramatically through AIDS awareness and prevention education." By the end of the ten-minute presentation, the managers committed to implementing an HIV/AIDS education program in their respective countries.

Include Ideas for Readiness. We also mentioned in Chapter Eight that help-ing clients and their organizations get ready for change is critical to your suc-cess. Be sure to include your insights about the organization's or group's readiness to undertake the implementation activities being recommended. Review the readiness assessment results and discuss the impact of those fac-tors on success. Include recommendations for ensuring that the client is pre-pared to move forward.

Position Recommendations According to the Audience's Opinion/Frame of Reference. Before discussing your recommendations, think through the PLOTs of those to whom you will be presenting. What language should you use or avoid? How can you best frame the recommendation to get agreement? What is the best approach to take—formal or informal, detailed or high-level? If you need to influence a variety of people, how can you position each rec-ommendation accordingly?

Tune in to "Station WII-FM." There is one "radio station" that everyone lis-tens to: WII-FM (What's In It For Me). You listen to it, and so do all your clients. You must tune in and listen closely if want to find out how and why your clients will make a commitment. This often means finding ways to make it easy for them to understand how your recommendations can be of benefit to them or to their organizations.

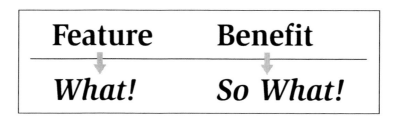

Borrowing from the classic sales approach, a key to influencing people is to translate the *what* (features) you are recommending into the *so what* (ben-efits or value). Features describe *what* you are recommending; benefits describe the *value* of the recommendation to the organization, primary client, or client groups.

Think back to the last car you bought. Was it the all-wheel drive and power steering, the sleek or rugged look, the dual air bags and anti-lock brakes that influenced you? Or was it the ride and handling of the car on the open highway, the way you felt sitting up high or low and comfortable in your shiny machine, the knowledge that you, your family, and your dog would ride safely? Most

People buy benefits, not features.

likely, you bought the car because of the latter. That is, you bought the benefits of having that car, not the features themselves.

Your clients are no different; they also buy benefits. So tuning in to your clients' wavelength—WII-FM—will help you be more aware of which benefits are important to your clients and will in turn make it easier to gain their commitment.

A client of ours who is a system engineer related this story about the perils of not tuning into your principal client's personal wavelength: "We were working with an MIS director to help him deal with a crisis situation in his company's system. For several months, we were fighting fires, solving problems, and keeping one step ahead. We thought we were meeting the client's needs and that he was personally benefiting from our solution to his short-term problem.

"One day during a meeting he commented that he was concerned that we were not getting enough accomplished. We sat there surprised, because we had "saved him," or so we thought. The more he talked we soon found out that he had also expected us to focus on the long-term solution while dealing with the short-term crisis. Senior management was requesting his long-term plan, and he was nervous about meeting their expectations. Since he didn't have a long-term plan he needed our help to keep his job."

Getting to the Personal Benefits

Use the following worksheet (p. 150) when considering the personal benefits your client will derive from your recommendations.

- In the left column list three recommendation options you will be discussing with your client(s).

- Next to them, write down the investment that you are asking the client to make (money, time, resources)

- In the right-hand column describe the *personal* benefit to the client and the business of each recommendation. Broad statements of benefits such as "save money" are not very helpful. Instead, think about what the cost savings does for the client as a person.

- The client's return on investment (ROI) is reflected by the ratio of benefit to investment. To achieve a positive ROI, the benefit must greater than the investment. While you may not be able to arrive at a

Personal Benefits Worksheet

	Recommendations	Investment	Benefit/Value
Option 1			
Option 2			
Option 3			

precise number, you can get a sense of whether the benefit outweighs the investment. If it doesn't, think of a more substantial benefit or a way to reduce the necessary investment.

Rework your initial notes into a script that you can use to sell your recommendations. This script is similar to an Expertise Statement, but the intent is different. You are not just trying to "hook" the client into opening his or her mind to new options; you are also providing specific insights and recommendations directly related to the project or situation that will require an investment.

We have also provided a sample worksheet (p. 152) to help you prepare to sell your recommendations. You will need to make the following final decisions:

- What is the goal of the discussion: agreement, approval, sharing of ideas?
- Do you want to present all the options, or just one or two initially?
- Which actions do you specifically want the client(s) to take? Remember, asking someone to take an action is the only way to test how committed that person is.

Writing your ideas down on paper will help you sort out the benefits that you want to focus on for each client. If you just wing it, you will tend to ramble and focus on features instead of benefits. After you have finished writing down the benefits you want to focus on, test your plan with a friend or colleague, asking whether the benefits are strong enough and appropriate to the client situation.

Prepare for the Discussion

The following are some additional tips to help you prepare for the recommendations discussion:

- Determine who you need to present recommendations to and whether you should conduct the discussion alone or with a team. Complete a PLOT on each person who will be attending. If people you don't know are attending, bring them up to speed before the meeting. At a minimum, introduce yourself and find out which areas they represent and their interests in the project. New members may require extra attention, as they have not previously been involved and therefore they may not understand the big picture or know the history leading up to the meeting.
- When appropriate, ask your primary client to be involved in developing and, if possible, presenting some of the recommendations. Consider

Selling Your Recommendations
to Gain Commitment

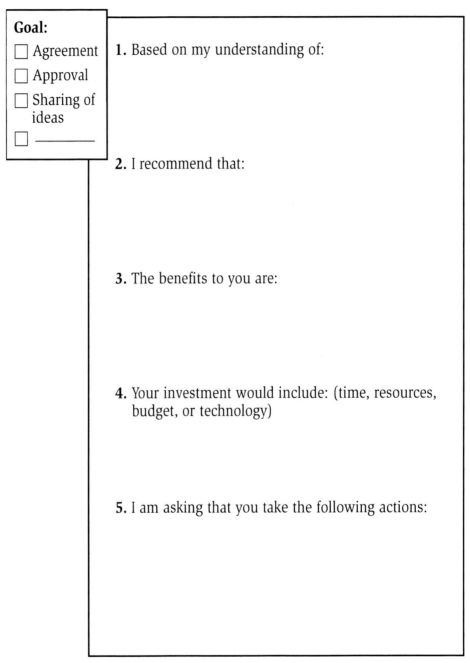

Goal:
- ☐ Agreement
- ☐ Approval
- ☐ Sharing of ideas
- ☐ —————

1. Based on my understanding of:

2. I recommend that:

3. The benefits to you are:

4. Your investment would include: (time, resources, budget, or technology)

5. I am asking that you take the following actions:

options, prioritizations, and ways of presenting information so that it is not overwhelming to the audience. When feasible, it is a good idea to include short- and long-term solutions. When you involve the client this way you are truly partnering. As a result the client will assist you when confronted with resistance from other client groups.

- Be enthusiastic and show your belief in the options discussed. Also be forthright about your concerns and areas where there is incomplete information.

- Prepare options within your recommendations. While you may have a favored approach, give your client a range of ideas to consider. You can sell your best solution by weighing the trade-offs of each, which will help the client feel more comfortable about the decision.

- Help the client to see the effort as an opportunity—not an obligation.

- Expect resistance and challenging questions during the discussion. Be prepared for such statements as "I don't see it that way," "It will probably be too costly," and " I think we need more data." "Peel the onion" and find out the underlying key issue. Remember that silence does not mean either consent or disagreement. If there is silence, facilitate the discussion to get at other issues or unstated assumptions.

- Include in your discussion the strengths of the group, team, operation, and organization, as well as positive results. Often clients do not hear about things that are going well.

- Do not name specific individuals who provided information, as this is a breach of confidentiality. One way to respond to this type of request is to say, "I told everyone that our conversations would remain anonymous, and I'm sure that if you were in their position, you would want me to abide by my word."

- Think carefully about what you hand out prior to the discussion. An agenda will usually suffice. Often clients take words written on paper as gospel. You retain more flexibility if you plan to send a summary following the meeting or if you write on a flipchart or white board during the meeting.

> *"You cannot antagonize and influence at the same time."*
>
> —J. S. Knox

Key Activity 2: Discuss Information, Insights, and Recommendations

During the recommendation conversation, you need to listen effectively and respond to questions and any resistance. To do this, you must be relaxed and confident. This in turn means that you must prepare not only for what you are going to cover in the agenda but also for how you will manage the discussion.

Even if you are conducting this discussion in a formal arena, your ability to be relaxed is of the utmost importance. The graphic below is a sample agenda to help you plan what to present and how to engage the audience to gain commitment during the recommendations discussion. The focus should be on dialogue rather than presentation.

• In reviewing the agenda with the meeting attendees, get agreement on the purpose of the discussion, expectations, time available, goals and outcomes, and any assumptions that should be included in the discussion.

• Once the stage has been set, share your findings and insights. Then stop and ask for reactions, thoughts, and observations from the audience. Be aware of people's body language. You will find out at this point if there is any resistance to or disagreement or discomfort with anything you have presented. Get as much feedback as possible so that you can determine how people are reacting to the information and options.

• Use the audience's feedback to respond and possibly to reposition your recommendations. This might necessitate omitting some ideas, adding new ones, reframing, changing time frames, or changing direction altogether. After you have presented your recommended options, take the time to discuss each one and its benefits and drawbacks. Again, use the Managing Client Interaction techniques of "peeling the onion" and paying attention to body language, tone of voice, and words to understand the client.

• Depending on the time available, try to get agreement and commitment to next steps.

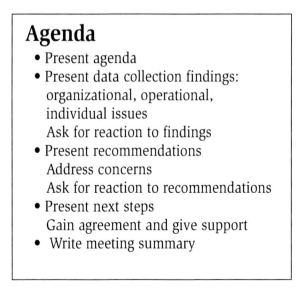

Agenda
- Present agenda
- Present data collection findings:
  organizational, operational,
  individual issues
  Ask for reaction to findings
- Present recommendations
  Address concerns
  Ask for reaction to recommendations
- Present next steps
  Gain agreement and give support
- Write meeting summary

Key Activity 3: Gain Agreement on Next Steps

Often, the time during meetings of this type is spent discussing issues, and then next steps are hurriedly confirmed at the end. In your role as facilitator, find opportunities to reach agreement before moving on to another topic. Capture agreements as you go along and review them at the end of the meeting. Designate a "parking lot" for those actions or topics that need more discussion and research.

A variety of obstacles can get in the way of gaining the client's commitment. Some of the factors that cause the lack of agreement are probably out of your control. Your ideas might be technically correct, and you might even have a change management plan in place to deal with the processes and people, but for various reasons—cost, inertia, lack of resources—the timing may not be right. The more homework you do up front, the more knowledge you will have about potential roadblocks, and the greater your ability will be to discuss ways to remove them.

Making Recommendations

This exercise will help you prepare for making recommendations and gaining agreement on next steps.

- Complete the Selling Your Recommendations Worksheet if you have not already done so.
- Complete a PLOT on each client who will be part of the discussion.
- Role play with a colleague the recommendations discussion and get feedback on how to make it more compelling to your specific client.
- Discuss the recommendation with the client and notice what factors enabled him or her to commit or which ones prevented the client from committing. Remember to "peel the onion" as you question to find out the client's personal needs, concerns, and other ideas.

CHAPTER HIGHLIGHTS

- The core of Phase 3 is to make recommendations based on information and insights gathered in Phase 2 and get commitment to what will be implemented in Phase 4. In doing this, focus on continuing to build trust and commitment, demonstrating flexibility, and keeping the process moving.
- Plan what to say and how to say it.
- Involving your client is an opportunity to presell ideas and to identify those areas that will be of concern.

- Stories, analogies, and dramatic demonstrations are powerful communication techniques for relating your observations from Phase 2 and from your overall experience.

- Be sure to include your insights about the organization's or group's readiness to undertake the implementation activities being recommended.

- Before discussing your recommendations, think through the PLOTs of those to whom you will be presenting.

- The key to influencing people is to translate the *what* (features) you are recommending into the *so what* (benefits or value).

- Prepare options within your recommendations.

- Expect resistance and challenging questions.

- Prepare not only what you are going to cover in the agenda but also how you will manage the discussion.

- Use the audience's feedback to respond and possibly reposition your recommendations.

- Capture agreements as you go along and review them at the end of the meeting.

- The more homework you do up front, the more knowledge you will have about any potential roadblocks to gaining commitment.

CHAPTER TEN

THE ROADMAP TO OPTIMUM RESULTS

Phase 4, implementing solutions and following up, is in many ways the embodiment of the entire Consultative Process. All your work from the previous three phases comes together as you begin to plan the rollout of your solutions. Phase 4 is the point in the process where you design your roadmap to success for your project, task, or assignment. It's also the make-or-break point for all your efforts up to this point.

You may have learned the hard way that no matter how good your solutions may be, no matter how well-intended your goals, if implementation is not done well, it feels like all your work has been wasted. The effects of poor implementation can be devastating: your organization or your clients may find unexpected delays and unacceptable expenses; your client relationship may be strained; your reputation or that of your group may be damaged.

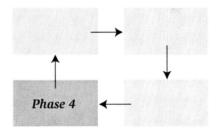

Phase 4

THE IMPLEMENTATION CHALLENGE

Why is successful implementation sometimes difficult? One reason is that implementation is viewed differently by different people. To some, it is the point when the organization can finally see some results—the system goes up, the hardware and software are installed, a new procedure is employed, or the training begins. For others, implementation is the "stuff that someone else does," devoid of glamour and excitement and invisible to senior management. And for others, implementation is a massive never-ending disruption.

> *"The hard stuff is easy. The soft stuff is hard, and the soft stuff is much more important than the hard stuff."*
>
> —The Milliken Company

Another part of the implementation challenge is the lack of consistent two-way communication between those driving the effort and those affected by it. Mary Jo Potter, managing director of Corporate Alliance, describes the problem in this reengineering example: "Organizations tend to look at the changes they are making from a structure point of view. 'I now want you to be my supplier. I sent a memo, now go do it.' The problem is that unless the change is communicated well, so that people know the 'why' behind it, it won't be understood. Ninety percent of the time the structure is communicated, but the essence of 'how will we work together' is not. There are many unstated assumptions and misalignments that directly impact success."

As people use more collaborative and team-oriented approaches, and as organizations leverage knowledge and expertise more effectively, perceptions are likely to change. People are becoming more aware of what successful implementation should be. The fallout from unsuccessful implementation—lost time, wasted money, frustration, lost opportunities to get new products to market, downtime, increased customer complaints, and bad press, to name a few—is far less tolerated now than it was before.

We asked our clients—senior management, project teams, and employees in diverse industries—what differentiates successful implementations from failures. They responded that projects or initiatives that fail have some or all of the following characteristics:

- No buy-in from all levels and client groups
- No tie to business goals or strategies
- No apparent benefit to individuals being affected
- No consideration of alignment between organizational, operational, and individual issues
- Are done to or for people rather than with people

How do these costly mistakes happen? Part of the answer is that the realities of implementation—the precautions, difficulties, and challenges—are not considered up front. Unless the thinking about implementation begins way back at the beginning, at the project's very first conceptual stages, shocking surprises, resistance, and rework most certainly lie ahead. This chapter is about using what you have learned from the beginning of your project or assignment to plan for and execute an implementation plan that produces the optimum result you and all your client groups desire. After all, you all have a lot at stake.

"It takes great courage to faithfully follow what we know to be true."

—Sara Anderson

THE CONSULTATIVE ROLES YOU PLAY IN PHASE 4

During the implementation phase you have the opportunity to demonstrate the breadth and depth of your capabilities by keeping things moving and providing insight and support to all client groups. The consultative roles that come into play during Phase 4 are the following:

- *Problem solver*—identifying and removing implementation obstacles before they become detrimental
- *Strategist*—linking implementation plans and activities to overarching goals and direction and providing leadership in communicating the importance of the project or initiative
- *Facilitator*—keeping the implementation process moving and the lines of communication open
- *Technical expert*—planning the best implementation strategy and ensuring that the right people are involved
- *Coach*—supporting client groups through the implementation process by acknowledging people's concerns and encouraging feedback and input
- *Influencer*—positioning the change to others honestly and realistically and providing motivation through the changes and transition
- *Administrator*—organizing and overseeing the implementation process
- *Partner*—creating a safe and exciting atmosphere in which implementation can be a learning process for individuals and the organization as a whole

KEY ACTIVITIES FOR PHASE 4

Use these three key activities as a guide for achieving your goals during Phase 4 of the Consultative Process:

- Key Activity 1: Consider organizational, operational, and individual issues.
- Key Activity 2: Identify readiness, rollout, and reinforcement activities.
- Key Activity 3: Develop the Implementation Map.

Key Activity 1: Consider Organizational, Operational, and Individual Issues

During the implementation phase, the challenge is not only to implement the "primary solution" but also to consider all the factors that will enhance your success. As you learned in Chapter Eight, the organizational, operational, and individual areas are important in developing a holistic understanding of the factors that will affect the success of the implementation. The information and insights you gained in Phase 2, by examining the organizational, operational, and individual factors with all client groups, will serve you well now, as you begin to plan the activities to implement your solution ideas.

Ross Stern, director of Human Capital and Operations at Arthur Andersen, describes the process he uses in planning for implementation: "One of the keys to assisting clients with implementation is to be able to adapt an implementation to the business, situation, and people being impacted. For example, instead of using a recipe, we need to know the specific outcomes desired and have a kitchen full of ingredients and spices. Based on the client need, I pull the right ingredients off the shelf to create an implementation that fits the client's needs, business, culture, operational processes, and individual skills and attitudes."

Tips for Reviewing Organizational, Operational, and Individual Factors

Start your implementation strategy by reviewing your learnings from Phase 2 for each client group. For each group, ask yourself the following questions:

Organizational Factors

- What are the best ways to communicate the link between this project or task and the vision, goals, objectives, and strategies?
- What obstacles can be anticipated based on the style, culture, politics, or human resource philosophy of the organization?
- Will growth, trends, life cycle of products, or competition have any impact on our implementation efforts?
- What change-management strategies do I need to consider to be successful?

Operational Factors

- What impact will implementation have on systems, processes, procedures, and distribution of information?
- What measures of success will be used to evaluate the project or task?
- Will any changes to performance management systems be necessary?
- What change-management transition plans need to be considered?

Individual Factors

- What skills and knowledge areas will be affected?
- How can attitudes and morale be improved and motivation increased during implementation?
- How will performance be enhanced during implementation and ongoing learning encouraged?
- What change and transition support will people need?

Key Activity 2: Identify Readiness, Rollout, and Reinforcement Activities

In working with our clients to plan their implementation strategies, we developed a comprehensive framework and step-by-step methodology for considering success and failure factors. This framework also integrates the elements within the Consultative Balance: working with people, using a collaborative process, and leveraging expertise. The organizing principles of this implementation-planning framework are the phases of readiness, rollout, and reinforcement. These phases represent a timeline for the organizational, operational, and individual implementation activities. Let's look at each of these phases one by one.

"Readiness is 'getting it.' Rollout is 'getting it going.' Reinforcement is 'getting it growing.'"

—Jeff Lucas,
Science Applications
International
Corporation

Readiness. As mentioned earlier, lack of readiness—of the organization, the operations, or the people—is a major factor in the failure of implementation efforts. This is because readiness is not universally seen as an implementation activity that requires focus and planning. In fact, some might say that readiness is halting the progress of rollout. The irony is that when readiness is planned for and committed to, the odds of meeting goals and achieving optimum results increase substantially.

The readiness assessment described in Chapter Eight is a great tool to help you decide where to target your energies and attention. It is important to recognize that immediately before rollout, every client group has a greater need for communication, information, and time to share ideas and concerns. The urgency, the benefits, and the consequences of any initiative need to be repeated in many different ways by many different people to everyone who will be affected. A single grandiose "vision" speech is not enough. Creating readiness requires constant organizationwide communication.

Creating readiness at the individual level is just as—if not more—critical. For implementation to be successful, individuals must see the benefits of doing something differently or understand the consequences of changing. They may not have a choice about what is being implemented, but they always have a choice in terms of their level of acceptance. Creating individual readiness by involving people in the process creates the crucial buy-in that greatly affects the success of the overall project.

How do people in your organization find out about a change effort or event that will have an impact on their lives? Probably with a memo or meeting with a manager, or maybe in a companywide video or e-mail. A manager client of ours describes the reality of his readiness efforts this way: "I get a big box on my desk. The letter inside asks me to review the contents with my staff by a specific date. I have no idea what it is about, nor do I have time to study the material. Usually, I slim it down from a suggested two-hour discussion to about fifteen minutes." A participant in a training class told us much the same thing: "I usually get a lengthy prework packet. Even if I get it on time, and I have the intention to read it, it becomes a low priority. I read it on the plane on the way to training or in bed the night before. If I don't get it done before the training starts, it usually doesn't matter."

Today, life at work is so busy that readiness activities become things people will get around to sooner or later, but often not in the way you intended. Obviously, the key isn't to create more work for people but to find opportunities to set the stage for and create excitement about the rollout that is to come. Helping people to understand the benefits—or the consequences—that await them is key is creating a state of readiness.

 Susan Bumpass, a senior manager at Arthur Andersen, describes one effective type of readiness activity: "Arthur Andersen conducts 360–degree feedback surveys as a way to create readiness in its executive development program. The feedback comes from the boss, direct reports, peers, oneself, and clients and reports back both the individual's self-perceptions as well as composite pictures of how he or she is viewed by others. This enables individuals to participate in a process involving reflection and discussions of these differences with their peers and coaches. The process culminates in the development of individual plans that result in enhanced relationships and higher levels of performance."

To implement any solution effectively, give yourself the chance to succeed by planning readiness activities to include all client groups. The following are suggestions for planning your readiness activities:

Creating Readiness Activities

- Realistically position the amount of time required: allow for a transition phase; acknowledge stress, confusion, and worry.
- Create anticipation and excitement to help motivate people to close the gap between their desires and beliefs and what it will take to create the desired result.
- Help people get a new perspective on the situation through various forms of communication, such as success stories and other anecdotes.
- Use different mental models and methods to engage people, depending on their level of resistance.
- Conduct activities so that people can get closure in transitioning from "the old way."
- Involve people in developing readiness activities that create awareness, understanding, and acceptance.
- Put in place support mechanisms that will be available to people during the rollout, such as hotlines, an employee assistance program, mentors, buddies.
- Get commitment to rollout from all client groups.

Rollout. *Rollout* is what most people think of as implementation itself, because this is where they see something happen. This is where the invisible becomes visible, and action is taken. The good news is that you can leverage this visibility by communicating successes to build additional interest. You can help people deal with transition issues, provide a role model for members of senior management that encourages their involvement, and, if necessary, make mid-course corrections. The bad news is that if something doesn't go quite right, everyone knows about it. The rumor mill goes into high gear, stories get exaggerated, and it can take a long time to recuperate.

Kristin Andress, a performance consultant at Arthur Andersen, was lucky enough to have an involved, committed client who understood that sometimes things aren't going to go perfectly: "We were responsible for developing and implementing a series of five workshops for our nontechnical training curriculum. One course was poorly received and was, to many of us, a personal failure. Our primary internal client, a line partner, had been involved throughout and was well aware of our implementation strategy. As a result, his response was one of a true business partner: 'Find out why it didn't work and let's fix it.' There was no blame, no finger pointing, and no admonishment. The fact that we partnered with him throughout and had a mechanism for making mid-course corrections enabled us to recover quickly when our pilot did not live up to everyone's expectations."

As part of your planning for rollout activities, consider these suggestions as ways to maximize your efforts:

- Position this phase as creating, reinventing, rewiring, or getting things going.
- Pilot new processes, procedures, and systems.
- Communicate successes to build interest. Create a story line that can be repeated throughout the organization and with customers.
- Create a vehicle for ongoing status reports and communication.
- Ask senior management to provide visible and vocal acknowledgment for changes thus far.
- Put in place a mechanism for making mid-course corrections with ease, and let people know it is a part of the implementation process.
- Create and employ a process by which new team members can easily be integrated into a client situation or team.
- Create an awareness of early signs that people are getting lost in the neutral zone: mood changes, sabotage, resistance, or elation. Put systems in place (EAP, hotlines, flexible scheduling, mentors, buddies) to address these signs as soon as they appear.
- Create temporary team leaders whose only task is to help out where there are problems.
- Include activities that move people from acceptance to assimilation and create a new way of working.
- Include opportunities for receiving feedback on the project, process, and relationship.

Reinforcement. Whereas readiness is too often relegated to the back burner, reinforcement often is never even considered! Why isn't reinforcement the high priority it should be? Why go to all the trouble and then not reinforce the outcome so that your client can obtain the best benefit possible? Unfortunately, the answers to these questions lie in the realities of work in most of today's organizations. After the new program is off the ground, people move on to a new assignment. Once the new system goes in, the excitement is over. Typically, quantitative factors, such as having met deadlines or budget requirements, are used to measure success. Qualitative measures, such as a program's effectiveness or achievement of intended results, are seldom considered.

So when we talk about reinforcement as part of implementation, we emphasize the importance of tying the aftermath of your hard work to the original goals and expectations. It is important that you and your client look at both qualitative and quantitative measures, fine-tune the processes used, and communicate successes and learnings to all who have a vested interest in the outcome. The key is to continue linking business needs to the organizational vision, operational processes, and individual competencies and rewards—and to do this throughout Phase 4.

When planning your reinforcement phase activities, consider the following:

- Position the phase as a time of measurement, learning, communication, and refinement.
- Measure and track results to determine actual changes and new applications.
- Build success stories and reinforcement of key messages into regular communication vehicles.
- Build a reinforcement plan that senior management members can weave into their normal routines.
- Provide additional coaching or consulting to individuals, groups, and teams to reinforce what they have learned or applied.
- Report results and learnings on a regular basis. Use graphs, charts, stories, and anecdotes to illustrate key points.
- Celebrate and recognize what has been accomplished and progress that is taking place.
- Create a mechanism for informing new team members, employees, and clients about the history of the change, accomplishments, and key learnings.
- Readiness, rollout, and reinforcement make up the entire implementation strategy. Taking time to ensure that all three aspects are in

place—and providing coaching, consulting, facilitation, and project administration—guarantees success and sets you apart as a true business partner.

Key Activity 3: Develop the Implementation Map

Now it's time to prepare your Implementation Map—adding your insights about organizational, operational, and individual success factors within the readiness, rollout, and reinforcement phases. We have used this mapping process with clients to create a comprehensive implementation strategy that takes into consideration the perspectives and concerns of all interested parties. The process is collaborative and generates buy-in, trust, and a high level of energy as people plan the details of implementation.

"Only those who risk going too far can possibly find out how far one can go."

—T. S. Eliot

The following story, told to us by Susan Gawley, a performance consultant at Arthur Andersen, illustrates how implementation mapping helped not only to build efficiencies, effectiveness, and buy-in but also to shift the team toward more consultative partnering: "We used the Implementation Map as a way to design our business plan and new learning strategy. The initial map was created collaboratively in a day. It included a great deal of detail; however, we wanted input and buy-in from the senior team. So we walked through the map with senior team members, got feedback, and made revisions accordingly. We continued to do this with different stakeholder groups and were able to construct a complete Implementation Map within two weeks that everyone bought into. This was a first for us in terms of input, buy-in, and excitement. We used this collaborative process as a way of demonstrating how we could work differently and efficiently."

The Implementation Map is designed to be used independently or as a collaborative activity with your team or clients. The process may take as little as a few hours or several days, depending on the complexity of your project or task. The process gives you the opportunity to identify challenges and support needs and to create a roadmap for solution ideas.

The map covers the following topics:

- Vision, objectives, goals (may be client, project or unit specific)
- "Red flags" or challenges within each phase

- Solution ideas (strategies, activities, tasks) to overcome the challenges
- A list of key clients whose trust and support you need and who you may ask to act as champions
- Key resources and support needed to complete the strategies, activities, and tasks
- Desired outcomes for each phase: readiness, rollout, and reinforcement

Creating the Implementation Map

To create an Implementation Map, begin by drawing on flipchart paper a roadmap graphic similar to the one shown in Figure 10.1. You may want to tape several sheets of paper together to get enough space. Post other flipchart pages around the room that you have titled as follows: Red Flags, Insights, and Solution Ideas. You will need to create three sets of these titled flipchart pages, one set each for the readiness, rollout, and reinforcement phases.

You will repeat the following steps 2 through 9 three times, once for each phase: readiness, rollout, and reinforcement. Write the responses for each step on large Post-it Notes and place them on the roadmap in the appropriate location.

1. Clarify and confirm the vision, goals, and objectives for the entire project or effort.
2. Write on the flipchart the desired outcomes for the phase being discussed.
3. Brainstorm a list of the challenges or red flags that need to be overcome during this phase. Use the categories of organizational, operational, and individual factors to think as broadly as possible. List each challenge on a Post-it Note and place it next to the red flag on the map.
4. Stop and discuss the insights you have about the red flags list. What surprised you, challenged you, or inspired you? Capture your answers on the posted flipchart titled "Insights."
5. List the names of key individuals and groups on separate Post-it Notes to remind the team to pay extra attention to these people in order to build trust and support, to develop champions, and to overcome red flags. Place these notes on the map in the appropriate spot. Discuss the PLOT of these people and strategies for how to gain their commitment and support.

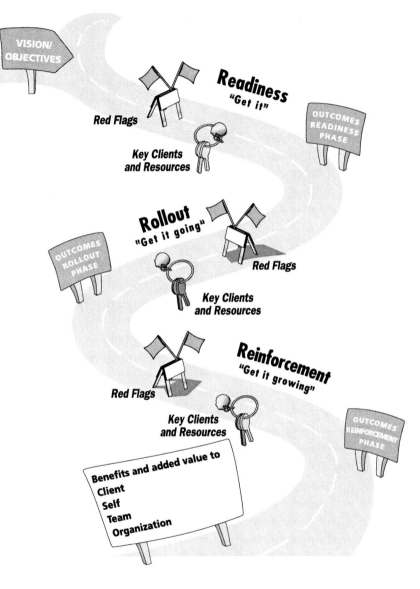

Figure 10.1. The Implementation Map.

6. Decide on the internal and external resources (budgets, materials, and so on) needed during this phase. Even though there may not be enough information at this time to provide specifics, develop as exhaustive a list as possible. Write the resources on a Post-it Note and place the note in the appropriate place on the map.

7. Brainstorm solution ideas (strategies, activities, and tasks) for overcoming each challenge or red flag, and post each solution on the map on the road for the appropriate phase. Again, consider organizational, operational, and individual factors that would help to eliminate the obstacles. As you decide on a solution idea that addresses the challenge, remove the red flag from the map and place it on the separate flipchart titled "Red Flags."

8. Stop and consider the following: If the solution ideas are implemented, would the desired outcomes be reached for that phase?

9. Discuss key learnings from completing the Implementation Map for this phase of implementation and list them on a flipchart titled "Insights." Transfer solution ideas for each phase to the appropriate flipchart, if desired.

10. Decide how to report back to other team members and client groups and get their ideas and commitment.

CHAPTER HIGHLIGHTS

- Projects or initiatives that fail have some or all of the following characteristics:

  —No buy-in from all levels and client groups

  —No tie to business goals or strategies

  —No apparent benefit to individuals being affected

  —No consideration of alignment between organizational, operational, and individual issues

  —Are done to or for people rather than with people

- Use the information and insights you gained by examining the organizational, operational, and individual factors with all client groups to plan the activities to implement your solution ideas.

- At the Readiness phase, find opportunities to set the stage for and to create excitement about the rollout that is to come. Helping people to understand the benefits—or the consequences—that await them is key.

- In the Rollout phase, leverage visibility by communicating successes to build additional interest. You can help people deal with transition issues, provide a role model for senior management members that encourages their involvement, and, if necessary, make mid-course corrections.

- In the Reinforcement phase, look for the qualitative and quantitative measures, fine-tune the processes used, and communicate successes and learnings to all who have a vested interest in the outcome.

- Prepare your Implementation Map, adding your insights about organizational, operational, and individual success factors within the Readiness, Rollout, and Reinforcement phases. The map is designed to be used individually or as a collaborative activity with your team or clients to generate buy-in, trust, and a high level of energy as people plan the details of implementation.

PART FOUR

THE PARTNERING STRATEGY ACTION PLAN

The chapter that follows summarizes all of the Consultative Approach concepts we have covered in the book, bringing them together in a single "action plan" package. The purpose of the action plan is to make it easy for you to consolidate your strategies for a particular client or client group. This enables you to increase the level of partnering between you so that collectively you produce greater results.

Realizing the personal and professional benefits of these approaches means that you need to practice some discipline in integrating the methodologies you have learned. Chapter Eleven provides a framework for that discipline and serves as a "one-stop shopping outlet" for all the techniques, skills, and processes presented in earlier chapters. We wholeheartedly encourage you to integrate these tools into your way of working.

CHAPTER ELEVEN

PARTNERING FOR RESULTS: YOUR PLAN

As we have noted throughout this book, one of the most important aspects of improving your client relationships is to work both strategically and spontaneously. The Partnering Strategy Action Plan is designed to be a living strategy document that evolves as your awareness about your client and your work together evolves. As you have more interactions with your client, revisit this action plan to capture new insights and plan options and next steps. The plan is intended to be used as a template, to cut and paste as you wish and as your needs dictate.

TIPS FOR USING THE PARTNERING STRATEGY ACTION PLAN

•   For each section of the plan, review the content of the corresponding chapter, paying close attention to the tools, techniques, exercises, and assessments included there. The activities and assessments in particular are designed to give you a moment of introspection in the midst of the tools and techniques. Your insights about yourself, your clients, and the type of situations your encounter will be of great value in completing this action plan.

•   Use the action plan to improve your relationship with any internal or external client (don't forget all your client groups: primary, financial, team members, coach, subject matter expert, and end users) with whom you are currently working or soon will be working. Complete the plan to identify gaps and areas to focus on in improving how you and your client partner.

•   Select a few sections to focus on. Make a conscious effort to apply those sections in your everyday work situations. Pay attention to any results or differences that occur when you use a particular technique or tool.

•   Complete the plan iteratively. At a given time, you will find that some sections apply more than others because of the stage of the process or your level of knowledge about the clients or situations you have chosen. As your knowledge and insights increase, revisit the plan to revise sections or complete new ones.

- Use the plan as a guide for team discussions about project and people strategies. It is also helpful as a framework for receiving coaching from a peer, manager, or mentor to pinpoint areas where you need feedback or input to stay on the right track.

THE PARTNERING STRATEGY ACTION PLAN

1. Partnering Comfort Factors (Chapter One)

Factor	Insight/Learning	Actions
Common Goals		
What results do each of you want to achieve?	• What is my goal? • What is the client's goal? • What is missing?	What actions can I take to define a common goal?
Common Values		
What is mutually important in the treatment of people and things?	• What is important to me in this situation? • What is important to the client? • What is missing?	How can I create more alignment on our values?
Open and Complete Communication		
Are issues between us resolved to both parties' satisfaction? Are we understanding our assumptions and how we arrived at conclusions?	• Are we comfortable sharing information, assumptions, beliefs, and feelings? • Are any communications incomplete?	What can I do to open up and complete our communication?
Trust		
Does each of us have confidence in the reliability, integrity, and honesty of the other person?	• What is contributing to our building trust? • What is missing?	What can I do to increase the level of trust?

Factor	Insight/Learning	Actions
	Commitment	
Can this person be counted on to fulfill agreements?	• Have we each made a commitment to the work? • To partnering? • What is getting in the way?	What can I do or say to increase the commitment level?
	It Works	
Overall, is there a sense of balance, mutual benefit, positive chemistry, and producing optimum results?	• What will we invest in this relationship? • Are we aligned, and do we find mutual benefit? • Do we produce optimum results in our work together?	How can I ensure continuing value over the long term?

2. Description of Client Engagement

- What are the goals for the engagement, project, or assignment?
- What challenges do I anticipate?
- What opportunities exist for me, my team, the client, or the organization?
- What are my goals for this client relationship?

3. Who Is the Client? (Chapter Two)

Client Name _____

PLOT

Personality: How would I describe this client's personality?

Language: What body language, tone of voice and words does this client use?

Opinion/frame of reference: What is this person's opinion and frame of reference about the work and about me?

Task approach: How does this client get things done?

P L O T

- Are there others who have worked well with this person in the past who can coach me on based on their own PLOT observations?
- What are this client's business objectives and concerns and personal objectives and concerns?
- What is our trust level? What actions can I take to raise the level of trust?
- What insights have I gained by reviewing my client's PLOT? What actions can I take to further the project and/or relationship?

4. Expertise and Value I Bring to the Engagement (Chapter Three)

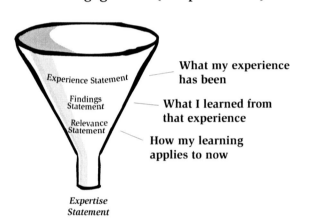

- What information and insights do I have that can help this client address business and personal objectives and concerns?
- Which consultative roles have I traditionally played in the past when working with this client and what were the results? (Chapter Three)
- Which consultative roles do I need to play in the future to add more value and to be seen as a partner? What actions can I take to make those roles more visible to the client?
- What opportunities do I have to make expertise statements that reflect my value?

5. Managing Client Interactions (Chapters Four through Six)

- What planned and spontaneous interactions will I have with this client based on the nature of the engagement and his or her role in it?
- What has worked well in past interactions with this client?

- What has not worked well in past inter-actions with this client?
- What challenges do I anticipate in future interactions with this client?
- How can I use future interactions to build trust and commitment and produce opti-mum results?
- Who can coach me on improving my interactions with this client?

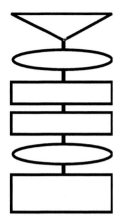

6. The Consultative Process: Phase 1: Create the Work Agreement (Chapter Seven)

- What do I need to know or do to understand my client's strategies, current situation, and needs?
- Have we agreed on roles, responsibilities, measurements, status reporting, review and input process, and clear objectives or goals for the project or engagement?

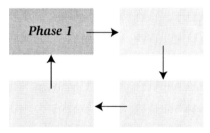

- Are any aspects of our work agreement of concern to me so that I need to address them with the client? my man-ager? my team?
- How can I use formal and informal work agreements to improve communication?
- What consultative roles will I focus on in this phase?

7. The Consultative Process: Phase 2: Define Key Issues and Solution Ideas (Chapter Eight)

- What information and insight areas do I need to explore, based on the nature of the work, client groups involved, and my expertise?
- What are the issues and success factors I must explore for each of the following?

  —Organizational issues and success fac-tors (Chapter Eight)

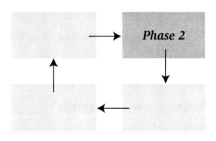

—Operational issues and success factors (Chapter Eight)

—Individual issues and success factors (Chapter Eight)

- What issues surfaced that indicated a lack of readiness? How will I discuss them with this client?
- What is my information- and insight-gathering strategy? What role do I want this client to play in this phase?
- What solution ideas do I have that I want to propose to this client?
- What consultative roles will I focus on in this phase?

8. The Consultative Process: Phase 3: Gain Commitment for Recommendations (Chapter Nine)

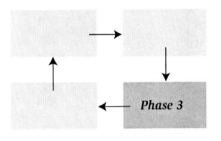

- Which clients are responsible for making the decision about my recommendations?
- For the recommendations I will make, what are the associated investments (time, resources, commitment) and benefits (end result, visibility) for this client to consider?
- How will I get buy-in and commitment to my solution ideas? What assistance will I need to do so?
- Who else needs to be involved in the discussions on making this commitment?
- What consultative roles will I focus on in this phase?

9. The Consultative Process: Phase 4: Implement Solutions and Follow Up (Chapter Ten)

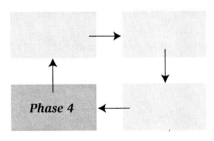

- What are my own and this client's concerns about:

  —Readiness (Chapter Ten)

  —Rollout (Chapter Ten)

  —Reinforcement (Chapter Ten)

- What is this client's role in the creation of the Implementation Map?
- What other client groups affected by this effort need to be involved in creating the map?
- How will the Implementation Map be communicated to all client groups affected by this effort? (Chapter Ten)
- What consultative roles will I focus on in this phase?

GLOSSARY

Anchor—A physical or mental technique of clearing your mind and immediately focusing all your attention on the task at hand

Benefits—the value your recommendation has from the client's perspective (see also *Features*)

Calibration—Gauging people's reactions based on past observations—using the tenor of their body language, tone of voice, and words—the same way you might test a piece of machinery to determine its baseline and then measure subsequent performance against that mark

Client—Anyone with whom you work: those you partner with, exchange input with, or need support or commitment from to do your work successfully

Client categories—Primary, Financial, Team member, Coach, Subject matter expert (SME), End user

Client interaction—Any encounter with any client (see *Client*), whether it happens formally in a conference room, occurs over the telephone, or occurs by chance in the hallway

Consultative Approach—partnering with others to produce optimum results and simultaneously build trust and commitment

Consultative Balance—knowing how to work effectively with all types of *people* while using a strategic and collaborative *process* and applying your *expertise* in ways that show your value

Consultative Process—a flexible four-phase process that allows you to balance *what* you need to accomplish with *how* you go about doing it, emphasizing both strategic and tactical aspects of planning and executing projects, tasks, and assignments

Consultative Roles—Problem solver, Strategist, Facilitator, Technical expert, Coach, Influencer, Administrator, Partner

Expertise—The application of information and insights learned from experience

Expertise Statement—Your experience plus your learnings and insight and their relevance to the current situation

Features—The actions or solution you are recommending (see *Benefits*)

Incongruence—Mismatch between what is said verbally and what is said nonverbally; mixed message

Listening filter—Preconceived notions, stereotypes, judgments, and expectations that influence what you hear and how you understand it—what twist you put on it

Mirroring and matching—Using your own body language, tone of voice, and words to reflect the body language, tone, and words used by another person

Partnering—Working cooperatively and collaboratively; building trust while working toward optimum results

Partnering comfort factors—Common goals, Common values, Open and complete communication, Trust, Commitment, It works

"Peeling the onion"—Questioning, listening, and observing to uncover core issues and concerns

PLOT—Personality (What is this person like?), Language (How does this person communicate?), Opinion/Frame of Reference (How does this person view the world, this project, and me?), and Task Approach (How does this person get things done?)

"WII-FM" (What's In It For Me?)—the station everyone listens to: tune in and listen closely to find out how and why your clients will make a commitment

Work agreement—an agreement made between you and your primary client or team members that clarifies understanding of what you will be doing, how you will be working together, and the results you collectively expect to produce; summarizes objectives, roles, responsibilities, resources, and deliverables; and ensures that there is understanding and commitment among all parties

RESOURCES AND REFERENCES

BUSINESS AND PERSONAL DEVELOPMENT

Arrien, A. (1993). *The four-fold way: Walking the paths of the warrior, teacher, healer, and visionary.* San Francisco: HarperSanFrancisco.

Bell, C. R. (1994). *Customers as partners: Building relationships that last.* San Francisco: Berrett-Koehler.

Bellman, G. M. (1992). *Getting things done when you are not in charge: How to succeed from a support position.* San Francisco: Berrett-Koehler.

Covey, S. (1989). *The seven habits of highly effective people: Restoring the character ethic.* New York: Simon and Schuster.

Fritz, R. (1989). *The path of least resistance.* New York: Random House.

Wheatley, M. J. (1992). *Leadership and the new science.* San Francisco: Berrett-Koehler.

COACHING

Kinlaw, D. C. (1993). *Coaching for commitment.* San Francisco: Jossey-Bass/Pfeiffer.

COMMUNICATION

Mehrabian, A. (1971). *Silent messages.* Belmont, CA: Wadsworth.

Satir, V. (1988). *The new peoplemaking.* Mountain View, CA: Science and Behavior Books.

Seashore, C., Seashore, E., & Weinberg, G. (1991). *The art of giving and receiving feedback.* Attleboro, MA: Douglas Charles Press.

Tannen, D. (1994). *Talking from 9 to 5: How women's and men's conversational styles affect who gets heard, who gets credit, and what gets done at work.* New York: William Morrow.

CONSULTING

Bellman, G. M. (1990). *The consultant's calling: Bringing who you are to what you do.* San Francisco: Jossey-Bass.

Block, P. (1981). *Flawless consulting.* San Francisco: Jossey-Bass/Pfeiffer.

Daniels, W. (1994). *Breakthrough performance: Managing for speed and flexibility,* Mill Valley, CA: ACT.

Lippitt, G., & Lippitt, R. (1986). *The consulting process in action.* San Francisco: Jossey-Bass/Pfeiffer.

Peters, T., & Waterman, R. (1982). *In search of excellence: Lessons from America's best-run companies.* New York: HarperCollins, 1982.

Robinson, D. G., & Robinson, J. C. (1995). *Performance consulting: Moving beyond training.* San Francisco: Berrett-Koehler.

Stumpf, S. A., & DeLuca, J. M. (1994). *Learning to use what you already know.* San Francisco: Berrett-Koehler.

Weinberg, G. (1985). *The secrets of consulting,* New York: Dorset House.

Weisbord, M. R. (1978). *Organizational diagnosis: A workbook of theory and practice.* Reading, MA: Addison-Wesley.

ORGANIZATIONAL CHANGE

Adizes, I. (1992). *Mastering change.* Santa Monica, CA: Adizes Publications Institute.

Argyris, C. (1993). *Knowledge for action.* San Francisco: Jossey-Bass.

Beck, N. (1992). *Shifting gears: Thriving in the new economy.* New York: HarperCollins.

Block, P. (1993). *Stewardship: Choosing service over self-interest.* San Francisco: Berrett-Koehler.

Bridges, W. (1980). *Transitions: Making sense of life's changes.* Reading, MA: Addison-Wesley.

Bridges, W. (1988). *Surviving the corporate transition.* New York: Doubleday.

Bridges, W. (1991). *Managing transitions: Making the most of change.* Reading, MA: Addison-Wesley.

Bridges, W. (1994). *Job shift: How to prosper in a workplace without jobs.* Reading, MA: Addison-Wesley.

Conner, D. R. (1992). *Managing at the speed of change.* New York: Random House.

Hammer, M., & Champy, J. (1992). *Reengineering the corporation.* New York: HarperBusiness.

Hammer, M., & Champy, J. (1993). *Reengineering the corporation.* New York: HarperBusiness.

Hammer, M., & Champy, J. (1995). *Reengineering management.* New York: Harper-Business.

Handy, C. (1989). *The age of unreason.* Boston: Harvard Business School Press.

Hyatt, C. (1990). *Shifting gears.* New York: Simon and Schuster.

Kouzes, J., & Posner, B. (1987). *The leadership challenge.* San Francisco: Jossey-Bass.

McCarthy, J. A. (1995). *The transition equation: A proven strategy for organizational change.* San Francisco: New Lexington Press.

Ray, M., & Rinzler, A. (1994). *The new paradigm in business.* New York: Putnam.

Schein, E. (1988). *Organizational culture and leadership.* San Francisco: Jossey-Bass.

Schutz, W. (1994). *The human element: Productivity, self-esteem and the bottom line.* San Francisco: Jossey-Bass.

Senge, P. (1990). *The fifth discipline.* New York: Doubleday.

Senge, P. (1995). *The fifth discipline fieldbook.* New York: Doubleday.

Watzlawick, P., Weakland, J. H., & Fisch, R. (1974). *Change.* New York: Norton.

PERFORMANCE ISSUES

Robinson, D. G., & Robinson, J. C. (1995). *Performance consulting.* San Francisco: Berrett-Koehler.

QUALITY MANAGEMENT ISSUES

Joiner Associates. (1988). *The team handbook: How to use teams to improve quality.* Madison, WI: Joiner Associates.

SELLING

Miller, R. B., & Heiman, S. E. (1987). *Strategic selling: The unique sales system proved successful by America's best companies.* New York: Morrow.

Rackham, N. (1988) *Spin selling.* New York: McGraw Hill.

Robbins, A. (1991). *Unleashing your personal power.* New York: Summit Books (tape and book).

TEAMWORK

Katzenbach, J., & Smith, D. (1994). *The wisdom of teams.* New York: HarperBusiness.

TECHNOLOGICAL ISSUES

Bancroft, N. (1992). *New partnerships for managing technological change.* New York: Wiley.

ABOUT THE AUTHORS

Virginia LaGrossa and Suzanne Saxe specialize in consulting to organizations on building business partnerships and integrating organizational strategies with individual performance. LaGrossa and Saxe have over thirty years of combined experience as internal and external consultants, marketing and sales professionals, product development managers, and educators. Thousands of professionals have attended their workshops from such fields as financial services, high technology, utilities, professional service, higher education, health care, networking, manufacturing, government, consulting, commercial real estate, and retail. Saxe has a doctorate from the University of San Francisco and has published articles on adult learning and instructional design in *Training and Development Journal* and *Performance and Instruction Journal.* LaGrossa lives in San Rafael, California, and Saxe lives in Tiburon, California.

INDEX

122; function of, 48; and gaining commitment for recommendations, 145; and implementing solutions, 159

Information gathering: on known/unknown problems and opportunities, 128–129; methods for, 132–136; on organizational, operational, and individual factors, 123–127; planning, 122–123, 136–139; tips on, 129

Interactions. *See* Client interactions

Interviews: face-to-face, 133, 135; group, 133, 136, 137; phone, 133–134, 135; tape-recording, 136–137

"It works," 15, 16, 17, 175

K

Kelly, W., 128
Kettering, C. F., 70
Knox, J. S., 153

L

LaGrossa, V., 78
Language, 29, 30; as PLOT observation element, 27, 28, 29–30, 175. *See also* Body language
Lao Tzu, 38
Lingvall, J., 20, 65
Lippitt, G., 95
Lippitt, R., 95
Listening, 57, 76–84; to body language, tone of voice, and words, 76, 80, 81, 154; to calibrate, 82–83; filters in, 77–80; for incongruencies, 83; to learn about situation, 80–82
Listening filters, 77–80
Longfellow, H. W., 92
Lucas, J., 161

M

Making the invisible visible, 142
Managing Client Interactions Model, 57, 144. *See also individual stages*
McKinney, D., 124
Meetings, goal setting in, 67

Mehrabian, A., 29
Metaphors, 89
Miller, R. B., 95
Milliken Company, 157
Mirroring and matching: to build rapport, 38–40; when responding, 90–91
Models: business process, 95; Consultative Process, 96–99; Expertise Statement, 44, 45; Managing Client Interactions, 57, 144
Musacchia, F., 24

N

Neutral zone, 130, 131

O

Observation, 6; of body language, tone of voice, and words, 76, 80, 81, 154; of client interactions, 36, 37; of clients, 26–37; as information-gathering method, 133, 135; sharing, with client, 90. *See also* PLOT observations
Observation track, 27
Olson, J., 89
Operational factors: readiness assessment of, 141; when defining issues and solutions, 126; when implementing solutions, 161
Opinion/frame of reference: broadening, 91; as PLOT observation element, 27, 28, 31–32, 175; and recommendations, 148
Opportunities, known/unknown, 128–129
Opportunity-driven partnering, 12, 13
Organizational culture, 11, 82
Organizational factors: readiness assessment of, 141; when defining issues and solutions, 125; when implementing solutions, 160

P

Parker, P., 137
Partner: assessing role of, 52; and creating work agreements, 105; and defining issues and solutions, 122;

function of, 48; and gaining commitment for recommendations, 145; and implementing solutions, 159; role of, 7–8, 9
Partnering: anchors for, 61–63; areas of awareness when, 35–37, 59–61; defined, 7; in the moment, 55–56, 59; types of relationships in, 12–14. *See also* Client interactions
Partnering comfort factors, 14–15, 17, 174–175
Partnering Strategy Action Plan, 174–178; tips for using, 173–174
Pavese, C., 56
"Peeling the onion," 69–76; example of, 74–76; in recommendations discussion, 154, 155; tips on, 71–73; when discussing issues and solutions, 132
Penland, L., 8–9, 130–131
People, 10; in Consultative Balance, 3, 7
Personal Benefits Worksheet, 149–150
Personal Gap Analysis, 9–12
Personality, as PLOT observation element, 27–28, 29, 175
Peters, T., 95
Pfluger, C., 27
Phone interviews, 133–134, 135
PLOT observations, 26–37, 37, 175–176; to gain commitment for recommendations, 144, 148, 155; and Implementation Map, 167; of language, 27, 28, 29–30; of opinion/frame of reference, 27, 28, 31–32; of personality, 27–28, 29; and planning information gathering, 138; and seeing three-dimensionally, 35–36; of task approach, 27, 28, 32–33; trust level dimension of, 33–35; in work agreement discussions, 108, 110; worksheet for, 28
Potter, M. J., 32, 157–158

Printed in the United States
148632LV00008B/5/P